2022

To Vanessa

You Fit Perfectly

TOPE TENIOLA

Thanks for your servant heart.
May you receive all that God
has for you, remembering
you fit perfectly in Him &
no-one can take your place.

Blessings

❧ Contents ❧

❧ Dedication ☙

This book is dedicated to a friend, whom I love dearly and wish the very best.

And to all who have been hurt and damaged by life's knocks, I pray this book brings you freedom from within and encouragement not to give up but rather to look up.

Acknowledgements

A special thanks to Elaine Dean, St Andrew's Church, Chorleywood; Pastor Ian Christensen, New Life Christian Centre International, Wembley; Pastor Stuart & Chloe Glassborow, Catch The Fire, London; Reverend Simon Rea, St Peter's Church, Edgware; Pastor Winston Bygrave, New Life Bible School, Wembley; Sister Helen Reimer, Logos Comunhao Chista Church, Lisbon; and my beloved son, Christian Walker.

❦ Foreword ❦

Tope has written an excellent semi autobiographical book on discovering God's perfect plan for our lives. Using the life story of Joseph as a back drop and her own experience from childhood to adulthood, she applies lessons from this great patriarchs life and that of her own in helping the believer to discover the perfect will of God for their own lives.

The book is filled with excellent biblical applications and insights into scripture that empowers the Christian to truly *'fight the good fight of faith'*. For example she uses the story of the men that gathered with David in the cave of Adullam (1 Sam. 22:1-2), to describe her own prison experience and the four D's facing the believer today: *Divorce, Debt, Depression and Despair'*, and how God used David to bring hope to these men who eventually became known as David's, *'Mighty men of Valour'*. We too through the help of the Lord can be the men and women of victory to which he has called us.

Tope's book is filled with scriptural references and many of her original songs and poems, which makes her book easily adaptable to be used as a daily devotion as one seeks to *'work out their own salvation with fear and trembling'*.

I commend this book to you and pray that as you read it that the Lord will give you a revelation in order that you will truly be *'fitly joined together and compacted'* and perfected by Christ's ministers to fulfill your ministry in *'the edifying of the body of Christ'* His Church (Eph. 4:12, 15).

Winston Bygrave
Lecturer at New Life Bible School, Wembley, London.

❧ Preface ❧

This book belongs to Jesus. If it were not for the Holy Spirit living inside of me and God's grace, I would not be able to write. I humbly step aside, so that God can receive all the glory. To Him be the glory, great things He has done!

Chapter 1

❧ That Stranger Feeling ❧

'Now Jacob dwelt in the land where
his father was a stranger.................'
Genesis 37:1

I do not suppose it is by coincidence that the first
sentence of the famous story of Joseph consists of the
word 'stranger'.

Stranger means 'unknown person' or 'foreigner'. If
I travelled to Antarctica on my own and set up home
in an Igloo, I would immediately feel like a foreigner,
unaccustomed to how they do things there. I would
also feel like a misfit; feeling misplaced and somewhat
uncomfortable with unfamiliar surroundings.

That was an obvious example. So let us take the 6th
of November 2009, when I travelled for my first time to

Nigeria, my country of origin. Due to the fact I had never travelled to this land before, I experienced a similar feeling as if I travelled to Antarctica, except of course the weather was hot.

The truth is, in the past, I have travelled within my country of birth (England) to do the everyday school run. Whilst waiting for my son in the playground of his former primary school, I have felt like a stranger, as though I did not fit in with the other mothers/parents. In fact there have been innumerable occasions when I have felt like a misfit within the land I was born and society I grew up in. For instance, within my places of work; churches I have attended; and among certain groups of people known to me for years.

How can that be? You may ask. Well, the feeling of not belonging or not fitting in usually comes from within a person. Yes, I know other people can reject us or make us feel uncomfortable, but it is only when we know who we are, that we understand completeness, we become securely rooted in whatever surroundings we are placed in at any given time.

Throughout this book, I use examples from the life of Joseph, which is one of my favourite stories in the bible. Josephs' character, in my opinion, is ideal when dealing with issues of rejection, offence, forgiveness and completeness.

The devil has come to steal, kill and destroy (John 10:10). His scheme is to do this as early as possible in a person's life. When Jesus said to Peter; **"Simon, Simon! Indeed Satan has asked for you, that he may sift you as wheat."** (Luke 22:31) I believe He was not only referring to a recent time before Peter denied Jesus, but He was more so, highlighting Peter's childhood. Peter had much insecurity, which stemmed from his childhood and caused him to be unstable (Simon means water or unstable). The devil knows that if he can rob us of our proper 'covering' as children (i.e. proper parenthood), it can cause a dent in our wholeness throughout adulthood. Here is Peter who was the only one out of the 12 disciples who was given the revelation by the Holy Spirit, that Jesus was the Messiah, being corrected by Jesus. Jesus knew Simon Peter's confidence at that moment in time was temporary. Jesus knew Peter was to become vulnerable and insecure once He was arrested. Jesus knew Simon Peter would feel lost at the removal of a fatherly covering over his life. Unless we receive healing and deliverance through the Father's unconditional love, from the pain and cracks of a spoiled or non-existent relationship with either mother or father; we will live our lives through a warped mind, which only knows rejection to mean we do not fit in or we are not good enough.

The devil is a liar and has been from the beginning. I myself take pleasure in exposing his schemes against God's beautiful children; that is, you and me. *People who know their God shall be strong and carry out great exploits* (Daniel 11:32b). And I pray that by the end of this book, you will be able to take hold of the plan God, our Father in Heaven has for you and run with it. Fulfilling your destiny begins with a dream. It is about knowing who God is, hence, who you are and ends up with a loud 'AMEN', it is done!

Let us first consider Joseph's background and character. Joseph was the great grandson of Abraham. God made Abraham father of many nations and he believed this before Isaac, his promised son, was even born. His faith was accounted to him as righteousness and he was called a *friend of God* (James 2:23). God promised Abraham that kings will come from him and we clearly see this in many generations to follow, through David and Jesus. However, little did Abraham know that a king was to be born as early as the fourth generation; a king was to be found in Joseph.

Joseph also formed one of the twelve tribes of Israel. The number twelve is the biblical number for government, ruler or authority. Joseph's name is written on the gates of the New Jerusalem, i.e. the Church (Revelation 21:12). When we arrive in heaven, we will see the names of Joseph and his eleven brothers written on the gates. Israel became established under their rule. Joseph was born to rule. Even in his darkest moments in prison, he had the angel of authority over him and the anointing to govern.

Joseph lost his mother as a child. Death was not God's original plan for His children. The enemy tempted Eve in the Garden of Eden knowing that sin would open up the door for death to enter our lives. When a parent is taken away before a child reaches adult age, it leaves a void in that child's life. Our Father in heaven has both mother and father traits. Our earthly mother and father when joined in marriage and sexual union, they become one. So while growing up, we feel secure and complete in them as a child, knowing the two are one both masculine and feminine. If a child born from loving parents, is asked by one of them which of his/her parents do they love more, that child will not be able to answer, in fact it may hurt the child to even consider the answer. I say this because; this is exactly what happened to me when I was about 3 years of age.

My father asked me whom I liked best between him and my mother. I first pointed to him, because he asked the question, then I pointed to my mother, who was in the middle of massaging my scalp (my favourite pampering), then I pointed to him then her, then him, then her and finally became so confused, I burst into tears because it hurt so much to consider it. As far as I was concerned I loved them both the same and did not want to have to choose. They both represented who I was as a child and I was secure in that.

Now when one of them is taken away outside of our control, that is a different matter altogether. Not only does it feel like you have been forced to choose, you become even more confused and you feel there is some injustice. It leaves pain, rejection and anger. It also leaves you feeling vulnerable with the tendency to carry deep insecurities.

I lost my mother *twice*: The first time was when, due to illness and by no fault of her own, she left us all to return to Nigeria. This was the last time I ever saw my mother. I was nearly 10 years old. The second time was when she died. I was 18 years old. I remember both occasions as though they happened yesterday.

I lost my mother when I most needed her. My mother was longing to go back to Nigeria to her family, while she was ill, so my dad reluctantly let her go. I remember standing in the airport waving bye-bye. Little did I know at the time that this wave would end up a farewell wave. As my mum walked around the bend through the terminal doors, tears rolled down my eyes and knots entered my stomach. I felt powerless to change things, too weak and vulnerable to know what to even say. I was at the beginning of puberty and remember my father handed me these funny looking large pads with loops at either end, which I thought were nappies, then he gave me a health encyclopaedia book to read about the women's menstrual cycle at the age of 10. I remember phoning him at work, feeling very excited when I started at 11 years of age, just before I started secondary school. I said "dad, guess what, I have my menstruation." I used the proper word and was very pleased with myself, but realising afterwards I had just embarrassed my father. I had to figure out everything else for myself from then on. My dad tried to put me in touch with my auntie but she had her own worries and did not have the time for me. On top of that I had to act as a mother to my then baby sister, who never knew our mother. I also had to blank out the sexual abuse by boys and men (all of whom I have forgiven), who took advantage of me. Overall my childhood was pretty dysfunctional to say the least. I have some good memories and some disturbing ones as well.

Somehow, I had hoped to see my mother again. My desire was to travel to Nigeria at the age of 16, with my father when he was planning to go. But those plans were frustrated and he took my younger sister instead. I was really upset but thought I would write my mother a short letter at least to encourage and strengthen her. I thought that we would all be a family again and that I would see her on the next visit. Two years later, we received news of my mother's death. I have to say to this very day; I have never been so devastated, with the exception of my divorce, which I will refer to in later chapters.

When I received the news, it felt like the umbilical cord, which originally joined us together in the womb, had been cut. I felt it being cut at the thought of my mother being no more. The shock and pain together caused me to scream out cries, I wailed out loud and then passed out. After that day, I spoke nothing of my mother's death until a long while later. I guess I was still living in denial. I never went to my mother's funeral because there was nobody to take me and apparently, she was buried almost immediately. Many years after that were lonely times for me. One can say, my hope of seeing my mother again was deferred. The bible says, "Hope deferred makes the heart sick." (Proverbs 13:12). I remember calling my brothers to hold a memorial service for her but that was not enough. I planted a tree in memory of her and have the certificate in a frame, but that was still not enough. I went for counselling but that was again not enough. If anything it made me feel worse. If I am to be honest, the true healing process only began a couple of years ago. That is about 26 years after I first lost my mother. That is a long time to carry vulnerability, insecurities and rejection.

The healing process began when the Lord showed me a vision, by way of flash backs of when He had intervened divinely in my life. During those memorable times, I knew it was Him and only Him. Then He said to me, "you have not received My love properly." Then He showed me again scenes of when He carried me or delivered me from scary or dangerous situations. Some of the flashbacks of these scenes are written as testimonies within this book. Then I saw what He meant and burst into tears.

I delved into the meaning of 'receive' and found that it is not passive but proactive. I realised I had to experience God's love before I could get healed. That was very hard at first because I was so used to giving of myself and not being able to trust anyone else fully with my heart, since my divorce. In fact it was a great struggle for me to be still and know that He is God. I thought it would be impossible for me to simply let go. Letting go for me back then included, not having to study my bible religiously in the mornings during my quiet times. At one point He did not even want me to speak during my prayer, but just be still and receive His love. This took some time but He eventually broke through and I just wept and wept on my knees under my blanket in that secret place, just the two of us, Daddy in heaven and me. Before this, I used to feel so guilty even when I was only tempted that I used to visualise myself weeping and clinging onto my Lord's ankles as though He was going to abandon me. I was fearful of the Lord's rejection because I had not known unconditional love. The true love of our Father in heaven became distorted over the years. It is only by proactively receiving His love; I have learnt to take refuge in Him.

Some time later, I eventually became friends with the Holy Spirit and He spoke to me and I spoke to Him about my true feelings and about the pain I was then undergoing by people who were hurting me because they were so hurting themselves. He kept telling me to forgive them because He is doing a work in me. Trust me, it is only by God's grace I stand. I now visualise myself in our Father's hand by a waterfall relaxing and being tickled by Him with His other hand; I laugh and laugh as I bask in His Fatherly and Motherly love. I no longer fear the rejection of our Daddy in Heaven. He is true to His promises and He never rejects His children (Psalm 27:10). He knows those who are His. [Please see my tips in the appendix on how to download the Father's love].

I have a picture frame in my home above my son's photo on his first day in nursery. It reads: 'Mothers hold their children's hands for a while and their hearts forever'. No one can replace a mother. Only the love of God can fill that void.... Only, the love of God.

So, here we have Joseph, for no fault of his own, he loses his mother Rachel, while he is still a child. None of his half brother's mothers were able to take her place. Joseph would have certainly gone through similar emotions as I did.

> 'He who dwells in the secret place
> of the Most High, shall abide under
> the shadow of the Almighty.'
> Psalm 91:1

The love of God sustained Joseph, which would have caused him to also love and care for his then baby brother Benjamin.

Joseph was the apple of his father, Jacob's eye. One could argue he was spoilt or sedated by his father, who bought him that famous multi-coloured dream coat (Genesis 37:3). I say sedated, because how do we know that part of the reason why Jacob singled Joseph out was because he unconsciously wanted to compensate for Joseph not having a mother?

I was also the apple of my father's eye when I was a child. This caused me to be quite spoilt and the 'tell-tell' in the family. I would always tell my father about the naughty things my brothers did or said (Genesis 37:2) and what anyone else said, which was suspect. My father won my loyalty and my love. I was very sincere to him.

When fathers especially, show favouritism towards one of their children or regularly and openly single someone out to be special among the rest, an unhealthy environment begins to emerge in that household. Other siblings and even their mother tend to become resentful. This may be subtle to begin with but at given opportunities, hurtful remarks may be made at the favoured one, or they begin to ostracise him/her. Some siblings, even the mother can become physically abusive. When favouritism is shown in any family setting, especially in churches where there is a love deficiency, some of the weaker ones open the door to the enemy. Most of the time, the father/leader is oblivious; but at other times they are fully aware of the contention and sibling rivalry he/she has caused and feels powerful as a result. This way the father/leader feels they can better control the family. The need to control is born out of fear and insecurity. And insecurity is born out of pride or rejection. I believe Joseph's father Israel (Jacob) was truly unaware that his preference for Joseph had caused strife within his family. He did not see his behaviour as selfish.

Joseph was the skunk of his brothers' eyes. They hated him (Genesis 37:4). To them, jealousy was not an issue. They could not hide their envy and anger. I believe parents should avoid where possible to show favouritism among children. God shows no favouritism (Romans 2:11). We are all equal favourites of His. I am not referring to being used according to our talents and faith; this is different. God chooses different people to carry out different tasks in order to get the job done. He wants us to copy this within families. Nevertheless, many parents have a favourite and sadly show it, without realising the other siblings are not mature enough to cope with the feelings of rejection. Even if the siblings love the one who appears to be loved more than them, they will feel left out and hurt. Most will carry these hurt feelings into adult life and try and perform better than others in order to get noticed. They will constantly strive until they come to truly know the unconditional love of God the Father.

This brings me onto to our next point. Despite being the apple of his father's eye, I believe deep down, Joseph sadly felt like a misfit. It appears he was desperate to belong. He was brought up by his dad among brothers who had both a mother and father upbringing. He did not know his mother, and more than likely was the one responsible for taking care of Benjamin because his father was quite old. This may have made him feel a little inferior. The truth is most people who are singled out from the so called 'rest', feel left out when it comes to getting on with reality. They end up with no one to play with. Others begin to see them as different and continue to get on with normal everyday life. Jacob had spoilt Joseph to the extent that Joseph was brave enough to even tell his own father his then seemingly arrogant dream. I believe Joseph had the gift of interpreting dreams as a child. He knew he was gifted but due to his own insecurities, coupled with his knowledge of being special, he went about sharing his dream in an unwise way. Not that he was incorrect, he simply lacked wisdom. We must be careful whom we share our dreams with, as we do not know what is in the heart of man. We must seek wisdom. Some have also argued that Joseph was showing off, albeit, in a naïve way. Nevertheless, he was being truthful – we all know for a fact, on hindsight, Joseph certainly did not lie about his dream.

I believe everyone at some stage of life, has felt like a misfit. Take a few moments to think back over your life; at the times you were rejected or felt you just did not belong, even if it was only in your imagination. Remember we live in a fallen world. Even Jesus, the Messiah, was despised and rejected. God in flesh was not immune from the wounds received by the rejection of humankind on earth. It is time to be truthful with ourselves. I believe God wants to heal all of us.

I can think of many situations in my past when I have felt like I did not fit in. For instance, during my primary school days, I used to feel like a misfit because I was the only black girl in my class at one stage. I used to be teacher's pet. Even the headmaster of my primary school took me up to his office to give me one of his personal plasters when I had the tiniest cut on my finger. I remember he let me sit in the large leather swivel chair. In secondary school I used to want to fit in with the girls who were disruptive in class. I did not want to be a goody goody any more because it did not seem cool. I desperately wanted to be cool. In the workplace, at times I felt different and when I went to collect my son from primary school, I felt insecure and as though I did not fit in with the other mums. The World is a lonely place when you do not know Jesus. The good news is, Jesus knows you and He is knocking on your door, waiting to be invited in. When you welcome Him in, He begins the healing process through the 'getting to know you' method. The more you get to know Him, you get to know His grace and you trust Him more day by day to do a deep work in you. I will mention more about rejection in later chapters.

※ ※ ※

Chapter 2

Dreams and Visions are here
❧ Today for our Tomorrow ❧

So he said to them, please hear
this dream which I have dreamed:
"There we were, binding sheaves
in the field. Then behold, my sheaf
arose and also stood upright; and
indeed your sheaves stood all around
and bowed down to my sheaf."
Genesis 37:6-7

Dreams and visions are given to us for a reason. (Joel 2:1-28-29). Most dreams and visions are prophetic. I have learnt that visions consist of a revelation given visually to a person's imagination while they are awake. This may sometimes involve seeing images that are presented to the eyes of the heart and often communicate God's word indirectly and therefore require interpretation. Some people refer to these images as being in a trance.

Some visions contain spoken words whilst some are silent. The Apostle Paul prior to his conversion had a vision of a bright light in the sky and heard a voice saying to him **"I Am Jesus, whom you are persecuting. It is hard to kick against the goads." (Acts 9:5).** The Apostle Paul could have interpreted this in two ways; either he imagined it, in which case the memory of it would quickly pass away; or he could conclude this voice was really Jesus' who was crucified, buried and miraculously arose from the dead and spoke to him from heaven as a sign. The second interpretation was the most obvious to the Apostle Paul because he was left blind and terrified.

When I was about 3 or 4 years of age, my mother took my brother and I out shopping in the market place. There was what seemed to me, thousands of people walking, talking, shouting and buying. I was quite a shy and timid child who never spoke to anyone apart from my immediate family and friends. My mother held both our hands on either side of her and I remember people, who seemed like giants to me pushing past us in a rough manner. At one point, some impatient people pushed through our linked hands, eventually separating us. As this happened, my mum and brother disappeared in the forward direction and I felt as though I was pushed further back. I could no longer see my mother and my heart sunk, that was it, I thought, I had lost her forever. I began to scream and wail like a baby. I was becoming distressed when suddenly I heard a loud voice say my name 'TOPE'. For a second I stopped crying in shock and looked over my right shoulder and up into the sky. I had to squint. There I saw an amazing enormous bright image. I stood there with tears in my eyes still watching what I can only describe as a bright light which was mainly white but contained the colours of the rainbow and within it was a figure with a face and I could see the outline of arms; and where the legs should have been, this bit stretched downwards as though it had no end or beginning. The face looked lovingly at me. Just as I was beginning to comprehend what was happening to me, I had another shock from the front of me, so I turned my head back and a little elderly lady bent over with a gentle and kind smile asked lovingly "what's the matter dear?" I blabbered my reply "I can't find my mummy," and then I started crying again. Within seconds, the crowd parted and my mother appeared with my brother. I must say, I was so relieved to see my mother again. My mother returned home still with two children, only one a little dishevelled. When I arrived home after settling in, great joy filled my heart, so I climbed up on my parents' bed and started jumping up and down as though it were a trampoline and repeatedly sang a song I made up, which goes like this: "I saw Jesus, I saw Jesus!" (Matthew 11:25). As I kept jumping I kept singing these words and my two brothers told me to shut up and kept pushing me off of the bed. I climbed back on and started singing again "I saw Jesus, I saw Jesus!" This annoyed them and they told me not to lie. Only thing is I was not lying, but truly joyful, showing off, excited like Joseph. Obviously I did not know the Joseph story back then. I had only attended Sunday school at our local Church of England in Norbury a few times. I have never forgotten this marvellous vision to this day. I remember it each time as though it were yesterday. In fact the older I get, the more the vision comes back especially at times when I require God's comfort. The only thing that baffles me to this day is, I always wonder if anyone else heard Jesus' loud voice call my name. Or did it sound like thunder like it sounded to those who were present when Apostle Paul received his vision? One thing is certain; Jesus is alive (John 12:32)! He knows our every need (Psalm 139:13-14). He brings comfort in times of trouble (Isaiah 40:1) and calls us by our name (Isaiah 43:1). Jesus said to those who believe in Him, they too like Him will have eternal life (John 3:16). I became a believer ever since this vision. At the tender age of 4, in my infants' school playground, I used to pray quietly to God, apologising for my wrongdoings. I knew His presence.

If you have been touched by my testimony and have not yet invited Jesus into your life but you believe in your heart that Jesus is Lord, then do not delay; turn to the back of this book and say the simple words of salvation to Jesus now. Salvation in simple words means, 'you are safe in Jesus' arms now and forever.'

If it is comforting you need, Jesus is right here with you. Do not be afraid. You may be going through loss or persecution right now and wondering when God will deliver you from oppression or affliction. Or you may be feeling lost, lonely, worried or distressed. God always keeps His promises. Meditate on these scripture verses:

> *...Under His wings, you shall take refuge...You shall not be afraid of the terror by night, Nor of the arrow that flies by day.*
> *Psalm 91:4-5*

> *I will lift my eyes to the hills – From whence comes my help? My help comes from the Lord, who made heaven and earth.*
> *Psalm 121:1-2*

> *"......I will never leave you nor forsake you."* So we may boldly say: *"The Lord is my helper; I will not fear. What can man do to me?"*
> Hebrews 13:5b-6

The beautiful thing about this story is 33 years later, when I attended a Church leaders' conference in Bogotá, Columbia in 2007, I met a beautiful silver haired lady in the swimming pool of our hotel. We spoke at length and she told me the late Derek Prince used to be the spiritual father to both her and her husband, who Pastors a church in Lisbon, Portugal. The next morning we exchanged details and she invited my family and myself to visit them in Portugal. She told me she had been praying to God ever since she arrived in Columbia to meet a Black English woman. She told her husband that same night that God had answered her prayers. We kept in regular contact. One day she wrote to me and enclosed a postcard of the most beautiful painting I had ever seen. When I looked closer, I felt goose pimples pop up all over my body. The top half of the painting resembled my vision in the market place. I was swept away in awe and wonder. I was so moved, tears filled my eyes, as I was reminded of my childhood vision and wondered again why the Lord revealed Himself to me and wondered whether my newfound friend, who had painted the picture had seen a similar vision. My friend's name is Helen, I call her 'auntie Helen' and her name means 'light'. She has been a light in my life ever since. Auntie Helen and her also amazing husband Jimmy are both missionaries and Senior Pastors, from missionary families. Auntie Helen's parents were missionaries in Swaziland and Jimmy's uncle was among the first 4 missionaries to set foot in the Amazon Jungle. Auntie Helen and Jimmy are now family to both Christian, my son and I. They are also our friends and spiritual mentors to me in my ministry. I have a lot to learn from them.

Below is a photograph of Sister Tope standing next to Sister Helen's painting of the image of Christ, based in their church in Lisbon. The second photo is a photo of Sister Tope and Sister Helen standing together in the Reimer family's beach house in Portugal.

A dream on the other hand consists of a series of images that appear to our imaginations while we are asleep. Many dreams are simply the reflection of episodes from the past, which spring from the subconscious mind. At other times dreams are supernatural in origin. They are used to convey messages from God. Through dreams God can speak to believers and unbelievers alike.

Most of my dreams in my adulthood, I cannot remember when I wake up. However, when I do remember them, I either feel a burden on my heart to pray about them or to speak it out, if prompted by the Holy Spirit.

Once when I was abroad, I had a dream of a particular minister. In this dream, he looked heavy laden with worries. He was sitting at a table, when suddenly sheets of paper in the form of ledger sheets, used for bookkeeping, fell on the floor. He also fell heavily on his knees in order to pick them up. As he began to gather the sheets together in a sort of hurry, one of the papers was magnified. I could see what looked like a profit and loss account (income & expenditure), which showed quite a large deficit. The dream then ended. I woke up puzzled and concerned. I thought to myself, "This can't be right because this man is always preaching prosperity and usually boasts at every opportunity to show off a new gadget." The dream did not match up to what I had been seeing in the natural. A few days later, when I arrived back to the UK I heard that same minister preach. In his message he confessed to his money worries. I was stunned. I sat there with my mouth open because I knew about it before but kept it to myself. I realised at this point that my dream was supernatural. In fact it was prophetic and God was starting to nurture me in the gift of prophecy. I have since learnt to discern the dreams I should speak out and ones I should simply keep to myself and pray about. Prophecy after all should bring comfort and encouragement to a person (1 Corinthians 14:3). The end result should be that person being built up or convicted about something in line with God's word. If we obey God and speak the word He has given us for a particular person, the recipient's life can be set on course so they remain in the will of God.

I had a dream of a couple arguing in their home. Their fighting intensified and the room, which looked like their living room was a mess. Papers and other bits were all over the place but it looked as if it was simply untidy to begin with. There were no physical exchanges but I could sense, this was no ordinary 'fight and let's make up' argument. As the wife stood near the window, the curtains caught fire and flames started gushing uncontrollably. The wife then walked out on her husband and the dream ended. I was leading a women's group at this time. I asked the Holy Spirit to guide me to all truth and if it is His will that I would speak it out humbly to the women in my group. So at our next meeting, I used an appropriate opportunity to speak out my dream, knowing the Holy Sprit wanted to do something supernaturally through me that would have a lasting impact on one of the married couples. Most of the women in my group were married so I did not know which one of them was represented in my dream, as faces in the dream were unclear. After prayer, one of the women, before the whole group, gave her confession. She said, "Tope, the woman in your dream is me." A few days ago, she had decided she had had enough and had resolved to leave her husband. The woman was one of those I least expected would ever leave her husband because of what it looked like in the natural. But God sees everything. I then was able to minister to her accordingly and she was able to reconsider. This couple to this day enjoy a fruitful marriage. All glory goes to Jesus.

> *Then he dreamed still another dream*
> *and told it to his brothers, and said*
> *"Look I have dreamed another dream.*
> *And this time, the sun, the moon, and*
> *the eleven stars bowed down to me."*
> *Genesis 37:9*

Now Joseph's dream seemed rather far-fetched at the time of him speaking it out. But we later learn his dream was a message from God and by him speaking it out, made it real because he believed God. I believe Joseph confessing the dream brought inner healing to his soul. There is something we experience when God Himself speaks to us. He affirms us through His Word in the bible and even through His messengers. But there is something special and powerful, when God's spirit speaks to our spirit directly. God is Spirit (John 4:24).

We are His spirit children (Acts 17:28). When we pray to God, we hear His replies, when we remain still; the truth of His Word manifests in our spirit to address something we are going through at that particular point in time. He knit us in our mother's womb, He knows us full well (Psalm 139:14). Joseph was given a dream that was not to materialise until about 20 years from then but yet, this was God's heart impressed onto his. God knows the end from the beginning. He knows our messed up state now. But that which He has begun in us, He will see it to its fruition. He will show us something through a vision or dream to bring comfort in our discomfort; hope in our despair and faith in our disbelief. Then as faith is birthed in us, He begins a big work on our character. He builds scaffolding around us as layer-by-layer; brick by brick new foundations are laid. Internally, we can sometimes feel we are going through a fiery furnace, as we go through inner struggles as well as the struggles the enemy brings. But God allows these to refine us. When we come out of the fire, we shall not be burned nor even smell of smoke (Isaiah 43:2). God is with us. He has to build our character in order for us to take on the tasks He has ordained for us.

When you read the Gospels, you will notice the authors often wrote words to the effect of 'this happened in order for scripture to be fulfilled'. The authors refer to the prophet's writings years before the confession became manifest. God has the master plan and is in control. He wrote the manual for our lives. He has set before us an open door and no one can shut it (Revelations 3:8). Our gifts and call from God is irrevocable (Romans 11:29). What He has written will be fulfilled in Jesus' name.

✵ ✵ ✵

Chapter 3

❧ Warning about dreams ❧

*So he told his dream to his father
and his brothers; and his father
rebuked him and said to him,
"What is this dream that you have
dreamed? Shall your mother and I
and your brothers indeed come to
bow down to the earth before you?"*

Genesis 37:10

Be careful who you tell your dream to, especially if it
involves those people and you knew it. Some people can
get hurt or offended by your dream and resent you for
even telling them. If the dream whether prophetic or not
involves something which sounds negative about the
others in your dream, take the dream to God in prayer.
If you are still burdened by the dream, it may be you
need to write it down in a journal or share it with Godly

leaders, so they can pray with you. Then leave it there and if it is written, that which has been proclaimed will come to pass. Only this way no one would be hurt or offended in the meantime. Wisdom is necessary especially when it comes to relationships. Joseph's father (Israel) told him off for making such a suggestion. Israel, as close as he was to God, was offended not because of Joseph's dream, because it is common for anyone to dream bizarre dreams, but because Joseph chose to speak it out. He confessed his dreams to the very ones who would one day have to humble themselves and submit to him. In many cultures, the younger has to respect the older and in all cultures the child has to honour the parents. To dishonour our parents is to dishonour God and hence a sin. I cannot imagine going up to my father in my youth and telling him, 'guess what one day you, Olu, Funso and Yetunde are all going to bow down to me.' Let us then remind ourselves what prophecy is for:

> But he who prophesies speaks edification and exhortation and comfort to men.
> 1 Corinthians 14:3

Therefore, we know that this dream from God was meant to bring comfort and encouragement to Joseph alone in a time when he was experiencing feelings of low self esteem. I believe Joseph was going through difficulties in fitting in with his brothers and was feeling very left out around this time. I believe his father not only saw Joseph as special but also recognised his needs to feel loved more than the others. So where there was no mother to love Joseph, his father overcompensated by giving Joseph gifts. This had a ripple effect in the family causing his brothers to become more envious and Joseph feeling even more isolated from them.

Why then did Joseph speak it out? I believe Joseph, in his excitement and as innocent as he seemed, may have wanted to prove a point to his family. He possibly wanted them to see that he was in fact worth something more than he perceived they might have thought. Joseph could have taken this dream to one of his stepmothers or gone to God in prayer. Joseph therefore showed signs of immaturity, rather than malice. Hence, we now can see one of the reasons, why he had to go through what he did, in order for God to build his character, before those dreams could manifest. Most people who confess a dream or word which has the opposite results of 1 Corinthians 14:3 for the recipient, speak out of either immaturity or malice. Some Christians, including ministers need to reflect on this point. Let us humble ourselves and continue to ask God to show us our hearts, so we can turn away from our sins. If however, you have been at the receiving end of a negative word spoken by a 'dreamer', it is equally important to nail any word not from God to the Cross and leave it there. Forgive the person and move on. God is LOVE! The Holy Spirit is so amazingly sweet and in love with us, He would not leave anyone feeling bruised or dishonoured after receiving His precious words. His words only bring life to the soul – enabling the recipient to move forward into their upward call in Christ Jesus.

Some dreams, which are prophetic, are meant to manifest in much later years. Beware of falling for first opportunities to live out the dream. Allow God to open the door for you in His timing, which is always perfect. About 6 years ago, I was given a prophetic word about my future marriage and family. I held onto this word, quite excited about getting married again and grateful to God for giving me this new chance to be used by Him alongside my Christian husband. About 4 years ago, I had a dream of my future wedding. The dream was short in length and I still remember it very clearly because it looked like one of the old-fashioned film pictures. I was sitting in my wedding dress in a hall where I saw guests including my son. In this dream, my newly wed husband was giving his speech as he stood up at the top table while I was watching him in the centre of the room.

This dream has not yet come true but read how I almost married the wrong man. Last year some women of God and I had been praying intensively for me to meet the man of my dreams and for him to propose to me before the end of that year (2008) and for us to have the wedding very soon after that. *The Just* shall live by faith (Habakkuk 2:4). I held onto this word and on the first day of October 2008 I actually met a lovely Christian man at a Barn dance hosted by my friend's church. He had also been praying to meet a Christian woman. From our meeting, he wooed me and we became very close in a short space of time. He said all the right words in the right places. He did his seminary for 4 years in Brazil and had ministered in various churches. He met my family and friends and all looked great on the surface. He asked me to marry him just before Christmas and wanted the wedding to be in January 2009, because he wanted a new start to his life. This matched our prayers and I was grateful to God for what I thought at the time He had answered. My pastors at the time were not going to be around on the first date given, so my leader suggested we get married on Valentine's Day. That date was eventually moved to the month of May due to complications with paperwork. Before May came around things began to unfold, which led me to fast and pray for one week, asking God for signs. I then concluded, although he was a nice man, he was not the man in my dreams and decided not to marry him. I now see the blessings of answered prayers where sometimes God is saying 'WAIT'. If God answered every prayer, the way we wanted, what a mess we would be in. We would ask for relationships that would destroy us. Billy Graham's wife, the late Ruth Graham once said she is so glad God did not answer her prayers to marry the men she thought she was meant to marry because then she would not have met Billy. God knows the best for us. Watch out for errors that can be made when holding onto a dream, which backs up prophecy. TEST all things.

How do we know that Joseph had not already in his subconscious, started to prematurely act the dream out?

> And Israel said to Joseph, "Are not your brothers feeding the flock in Shechem? Come, I will send you to them." So he said to him, "Here I am."
> Genesis 37:13

I sense Israel was indignant to see Joseph not helping his brothers as he should have been. While his brothers were working for the family, Joseph seemed as though he was skiving. Even if his brothers had deliberately left him out, he was acting as though he did not need to work or as though he was too good to be with his brothers in their lowly positions. After all, one day, they will all be bowing down to him. Israel had to immediately assert his authority to ensure Joseph did not think too highly of himself and start to boss everyone around. Joseph's reply, "here I am," has the appearance of boldness, but I believe deep down inside he was crumbling at the thought of facing his brothers. Joseph knew his self-righteous behaviour had gone too far and he was the end product of a hate campaign. The strife between these brothers seemed to go over Israel's head. He had no idea how bitter his other sons were towards Joseph. If he did he would not have sent Joseph out alone. It was as though he was sending his precious lamb to the wolves. Israel was oblivious to the fact that his sons had poison within their hearts because of his love and favouritism shown to Joseph. But when there is jealousy and hatred in the air, the hated person, especially if they are sensitive to the Spirit, knows it only too well. I have experienced this before; it is not a comfortable feeling. You sense something evil is about to happen but you may not be aware when and how it may happen but you know it is around the corner because it smells. Jealousy and hatred are unclean spirits within a person. If you sense you are on the receiving end start to pray. Depending on the situation and if there is time, ask other trusted believers to also pray for you. Put on your full armour (Ephesians 6:10-18) daily and cover yourself with the blood of Jesus.

> *For He shall give His angels charge*
> *over you. To keep you in all your ways.*
> *Psalm 91:11*

I will talk about 'angels' in later chapters. At this point, I just want to encourage the reader. You are safe in Jesus' arms. Violence is never justified in believers. The Spirit of the living God lives within us and the bible clearly says:

> *Let all bitterness, wrath, anger,*
> *clamour, and evil speaking be put*
> *away from you, with all malice.*
> *Ephesians 4:31*

> *If it is possible, as much as it depends*
> *on you, live peaceably with all men.*
> *Romans 12:18*

> *Do not say, "I will recompense evil";*
> *wait for the Lord, and He will save you.*
> *Proverbs 20:22*

> *Do not be overcome by evil,*
> *but overcome evil with good.*
> *Romans 12:21*

If someone close to you is behaving ungodly towards you to the point of malice, and you are really hurting, go to him or her and show them their sin. If they refuse to listen or are unrepentant, take someone else with you. If still they do not want to listen, take it to the church (leadership). (Matthew 18:15-17). Now if the situation is awkward and the one doing the malice is in the leadership and there is no real accountability within that church, pray to God and ask for direction. He will guide you. If He requires you to leave that church, He will send you to a church where you can flourish and reach your full potential in Christ, without the strife. And He will do it in such a way, that all parties involved are honoured. The Lord knows all of our weaknesses and will not give us more than we can bear (1 Corinthians 10:13).

There is no excuse to open the door to the enemy and seek revenge. There is no excuse for verbal or physical violence, or murder.

> *Let us therefore come boldly to the throne of grace, that we may obtain mercy and find grace to help in our time of need.*
> *Hebrews 4:16*

The good news is, when we repent of our evil thoughts, words and acts God immediately forgives us. If this is what you need to do now, take some time and find a quiet place to do this. It is between you and God unless you want to confess it to someone. There is healing in confessing our sins and much freedom when we repent.

Another reason why Joseph would have been apprehensive to ask his brothers if he could join them in feeding the flock is because he was unsure of the time for the dream to come to pass. Joseph may not have been mature enough to understand this or patient enough to wait. Little did he know God was about to allow an evil act of his brothers to lead him to a place away from their strife and into different places where He could begin years of rigorous work on Joseph's character.

※ ※ ※

Chapter 4

Dreams meant for Warning

And his brothers envied him, but his father kept the matter in mind.

Genesis 37:11

Then the Lord answered me and said:"Write the vision and make it plain on tablets, that he may run who reads it. For the vision is yet for an appointed time; but at the end it will speak, and it will not lie. Though it tarries, wait for it; because it will surely come, it will not tarry."

Habakkuk 2:6

Joseph's dream is a typical example of advising someone especially in his position to write it down. After writing it down, he could have regularly gone back to read it, which would have brought comfort, encouragement and edification to his spirit. Joseph's dream was not just for his benefit, but for the benefit of multitudes.

So I want to share a dream I had on Monday, the 27th of July 2009. This was the night before I was due to travel to Sorrento, Italy for a holiday. My son had already gone before me to stay with friends. I was sleeping and dreamt a peculiar dream and woke up burdened by it. I saw a misty or foggy looking hill. On this hill were many lamps burning. I felt as though I was in a place where a graveyard was very close by but I could not see the gravestones. The reason why I say the dream was peculiar is because the lights that were burning appeared fake. That is, they were not true lights but counterfeits. Then I suddenly heard a voice say: "The antichrist is here." Then the dream ended.

When I woke up, I remembered the dream and was burdened by it. I wrote the dream down when I was in the aeroplane on my way to Naples. My friend told me she lived in Sorrento but little did I know her actual address is in a small village off Sorrento called Torca. When I arrived I told my friend the dream but made no mention of my feeling of a graveyard close by. She went into deep thought. Obviously I had no idea why I was telling her as, it was not as though I thought she could shed some insight on my weird dream. Then to my surprise she told me that about a mile away there is a graveyard, which fits the exact description of my dream. I was shocked. Then a couple of days later, she showed me the graveyard during the night. The hill did indeed have lamps on it and the graveyard was at the bottom. The place resembled my dream. I prayed quietly to myself as we walked past. A few days later, I sensed it may be possible the antichrist could appear in the form of a woman.

For those who have read the book of Revelations, we know that the antichrist's coming is imminent, so this revelation is nothing new. However, this may be a sign that the end time is sooner than we expect. Did Jesus Christ not have to grow up somewhere? Who knew apart from God, Nazareth would become His hometown? Jesus came so that we might have life abundantly but the antichrist has come to steal, kill and destroy. He/she will start off subtle and before we know it, people will be receiving 'the mark' (Revelation 13:16-18).

Noah warned the people but they just laughed at him; the prophets of old warned the people and they were ignored and treated with contempt; the apostles warned the people but they were persecuted and martyred. How long must we fall on deaf ears?

> *"Take heed, watch and pray; for you*
> *do not know when the time is..............*
> *What I say to you, I say to all: 'Watch!'"*
> *Mark 13:33,37*

If your church is sleeping, wake the people up. If your church is a cruise ship, turn it into a life boat by going on the streets, into cafes, into marketplaces, schools, workplaces, prisons and other parts of the community including the underworld, where people need to hear the Gospel. If people will not come to church, take the Gospel message to where they are. Time is running out. We can no longer be selfish but selfless, regardless of how we look to others or what others say about us.

> *He who has an ear, let him hear.*
> *Revelations 13:9*

Some Christians, especially new converts and those carrying out their high call will experience attacks from the enemy whilst dreaming. Some have experienced a demonic presence in the room or demonic interference around their bodies. I believe the angels in the spiritual realm are constantly fighting on our behalf. Do not be naive in thinking demons do not exist. These could be manifestations of the battle between the angels in the heavenly realm and principalities in the evil realm. Read the book of Daniel. If you experience something like this, as I have, do not be frightened; just say the name of Jesus as many times as necessary until the evil presence has gone. Jesus' name is a strong tower; when you call upon Him, you are safe. Do not focus on evil but on good. Fix your eyes on Jesus. Jesus already has the victory. So keep dreaming dreams and discern the ones meant for speaking out, praying about and for warning. God will bless you.

* * *

Chapter 5

❧ Wandering Wilderness ❧

Now a certain man found him, and there he was wandering in a field.

Genesis 37:15a

When we think we know it all, we could adopt a false superiority complex. We become self-righteous in our ways. Our hearts become hardened towards everyone including God. Pride sets in and if we are not careful, we can slip into a time of denying Jesus. Haughtiness says to God, "I do not need You." Why do you think God allowed His people to wander in the desert for 40 years, when it should have taken them 14 days to get to the Promised Land? They were walking around in circles and they did not even know it (Deuteronomy 8). This was a good opportunity for His people to take a real good look at themselves. It was time for them to search their hearts. After God's people had the privilege of witnessing some of the most amazing signs and wonders ever recorded in history, they still rebelled against God and decided to go their own way. For Joseph personally, his dream symbolised the Promised Land. He was unable to claim it easily, hence like the Israelites' experience, a period in the wilderness with idols was necessary to discipline him. Do you have a desperate desire for power or fame? Idols can be anything from being hooked on TV programmes/soaps, to addictions to nicotine or drugs. Where idolatry dominates our lives, you find a period of wilderness. However, as long as you do not bow down to idols you will see your promised land.

When I was 12 years old, my father started to attend a Celestial Church. The leaders asked my father to be a leader within a matter of months and were pressurising him to give large amounts of money. I did not feel comfortable in this church as I saw strange things, heard strange doctrine and I did not find the people friendly. One evening, after my sister and I had fallen asleep, my father put the candle they gave him to light in our bedroom whilst we slept. I used to share a bedroom with my younger sister, who was 4 years old at the time. My father put the long white candle they gave him on a large tray in the centre of my room, turned off the light and went to sleep in his bedroom next door.

It was a well-known fact that I was the heaviest sleeper in my family. As a joke, my father once put two loud alarm clocks in my room, so I had to get out of my bed in order to turn off the second alarm, which went off about a minute after the first. That is how hard it was to wake me up. However, on the night of this candle burning, I miraculously woke up in the middle of the night; my eyes flew wide open and I quickly jumped out of my bed to see my room ablaze with fire and filled with smoke. I wanted to get my sister who was still sleeping (and she the light sleeper in the family) but I could not see her bed due to the thick smoke. I quickly ran across to my father's bedroom, which was also filled with thick smoke and patted him shouting, "Daddy, daddy the house is on fire!" My father jumped up in haste and saw the fire in my room and jumped through to pick up my sister from her bed and flew down the stairs to put her in the living room. My brother, Funso, who also was a light sleeper was still sleeping in his bedroom downstairs and so was oblivious to what was going on. My father filled up a bucket with water and ran upstairs to attempt to put the fire out. After much effort the fire went out but the whole house was dense with heavy black smoke and by now we were all coughing. My father opened the windows and we waited downstairs in shock until morning. Every time we blew our nostrils, black soot appeared on the tissue. When my father took us all to our local doctor, he looked at us and made some tests and said, "you were very lucky, if the fire didn't kill you, the smoke would certainly have done." When we returned home, my dad grabbed me and hugged me so tight, I could barely breathe. He broke down and cried floods of tears and kept rocking me on his lap calling me 'Jesus,' or at least he kept saying the words Jesus to me. I obviously at the time did not realise what I had done. Later that week, aunties, uncles, cousins were phoning to praise me. I felt strange and different. Then when we returned to that church, people were staring at me, a few even gave me dirty looks. I was so glad when my dad left that church not long afterwards. We must be careful which church we attend. Just because people gather and call themselves 'church' does not mean they are authentic. Test the spirits (1 John 4:1). My father celebrated Jesus that day after witnessing such a miracle. He knew all my life it had been impossible for me to wake up without loud continuous noises. He knew God's hand was upon us and used me to save the whole family from death. I now know that God's angel woke me up by opening my eyelids to see danger and caused me, who used to be a deep sleeper and afraid of the dark to rise up out of boldness in the dark and get help. What is impossible for man is possible for God! Hallelujah – praise the Lord!

Why then do we as God's people, like the whole of Israel, quickly forget the signs and wonders, the miracles that demonstrate there is a God who truly loves us? Why do we choose to go our own way? During my early teens, it was not cool to be seen as a 'goody goody' in the secondary school I attended. I remember my father tried to put me into a different school but I refused to leave because I had already made friends. I was quiet and submissive to begin with. There were a couple of girls in my class who joked a lot during the lesson and I became easily distracted. I would laugh at their humour and forget I was in a learning environment. When we eventually were split up into option groups, I was able to focus in the classes which they didn't attend and do well. However, during break times, we hung out together in a group and acted silly most of the time. I no longer attended church services and soon forgot my 'First Love'. I forgot the close relationship I had with God in my tender years and went my own way. I did not care when I was late to lessons; I tried smoking; thankfully did not like the taste of smoke; I tried drinking alcohol and getting drunk for the fun of it; I tried boys without full intercourse but there was oral sex, which I was misled into thinking was ok. I also got involved in a couple of fights; the first one was self defence after an older girl out the blue, jumped on me from behind and grabbed my hair and started banging my head with great force against a brick wall. I had no choice but to try my best to turn around and grab her hair. We stood in this posture for quite a while. The second fight was revenge. When I saw a gang fight already taking place with that same girl who attacked me from behind involved, I headed straight for her and started to punch her. I remember wanting to hurt her as much as she had hurt me several weeks before. Most wars in this world come from hurt, fear and a lack of forgiveness for those who have hurt us. Our hearts become hard and we open the door to the demons of anger, hate and murder. On hindsight, I remember an older girl in our school who warned us not to become a posse (named gang), no matter how small because it would attract trouble. She was right.

I have had a total of 3 physical fights in my entire life. The very first one was when I was about aged 10 in primary school. It was totally out of character. I saw a new girl who was hefty in size and whom I considered to be ugly. She had a serious and hard look on her face; she also had a very heavy African accent, which I felt ashamed of. I thought, "if the others here make fun of black people regardless of whether they speak with an English accent or not, what are they going to do to you?" I really did not like her. She reminded me of everything I was ashamed of about my heritage. Being a black girl growing up in England, I was never taught anything beautiful about the country or continent from which my parents were born. I saw poverty, suffering and inferiority all over that girl. So I pushed her when we were standing in the queue to return to our classes after playtime. To my surprise, she pushed me back and was very strong, so I hit her and the fight begun. I look back now very ashamed and remorseful of my behaviour. I guess I was feeling superior and at the same time confused inside. This is a classic example of the 'rejected' becoming the 'rejector'. I myself felt like a misfit and saw a vulnerable person who reminded me of how I felt deep inside.

This type of behaviour, even in a 10 year old has become a vicious cycle in society since Cain and Abel. I hated what I saw on the news about Africa or read in papers or heard at school. I hated when my father used to thread my hair so it was spiky and others stared and some laughed, including my brothers who used to call me spider woman. The struggle is on the inside of us. Today, I now sponsor a young girl aged 5 in Africa who has an even greater look of pain and suffering in her eyes, than the girl I pushed in primary school. I believe daily suffering does not give them a reason to smile, so their hearts become hardened and this is portrayed on their faces, especially in their eyes. When I look at the photograph of the child I sponsor, I want to do something that will put joy and hope in her heart, hence a smile on her face and ultimately great laughter. I want to see her eyes light up and sparkle like my son's eyes when he was her age. Her life is worth it. I pray Jesus will reign in her heart. I know only love can do this. God is Love. Out of love we are compelled to give and help the suffering around the world. When we in the Western world say we are starving, we have no idea how insulting those words would be to a suffering person in a third world country, who does not know where their next meal is going to come from and who die from poverty-related causes every three seconds. Many pack themselves on boats hoping to find a new start in a developed country. Some succeed like the young African girl, I stupidly hit in primary school. Most do not succeed and die along the way, forgotten or unknown, while the rest of the world is oblivious to their suffering. Yes, God is indeed our ultimate Source (Psalm 94:19), but how about those who do not know God and on top of that do not have a government welfare system? There are many things we take for granted in the Western world, even when our economy is in a mess. Please Lord; forgive me for my hardened heart. Those of us, who have received God's love, must do our best to bring the Father's love to the broken and destitute in our land and further afield, wherever our God sends us.

As a teenager, I was vain. I used vulgar words to impress my friends and danced with them to vulgar music. Believe it or not, while I was doing all these ungodly acts, not one felt right. Neither did I feel I belonged to the group I moved around with. Deep down, I felt like a misfit. At the age of 16, I thought I was a grown up woman and disrespectfully asked my father for my childhood savings he was keeping safe for each of us until we became adults. I think back now and laugh at my stupid behaviour, as I cried like a baby proclaiming and insisting I was an adult at 16 years of age. I have shared this story when I used to teach the youth church on the topic of honouring parents. I now have a wonderful teenage son and I can feel for my father. "O Lord, remember not the sins of my youth!"

A couple of months after leaving secondary school, I remember bumping into one of my old school mates on the streets. I have changed her name to Jasper for the purpose of this book. We reminisced together over what seemed like old times. She was very in with the lads and told me something that really impacted me. She told me about the time when there were two big fights outside of school. I was in my penultimate year in secondary school and word got around I liked a particular boy who was very popular among the girls and he had a soft spot for me too. My other two friends also liked two different boys. Well the boys were in the year above us, and the girls in their same year did not like us. In fact they wanted to rip us apart. I must confess, I was quite scared and by this time I had had enough of what seemed like strife and contention in our school. By now, because I was chosen to take my Mathematics and Statistics CSE exams early, I just wanted to face my studies and mind my own business but still keeping my main friends. I often wondered if I should have obeyed my father and gone to the other secondary school. But the spirit of violence was looming, where the headmaster failed to keep order. Word got around that a particular girl in the year above us wanted my blood. I did not know this girl, I had only seen her around the school. This girl obviously was in love with the boy whom I liked. I had been oblivious to this at the time. The other two girls in the year above wanted to beat up my two closest friends. Again I do not believe they were aware why. I remember there were about 60 or more boys and girls who turned up to watch the fight. Due to the big build up, you would have thought there was going to be a boxing match or a riot. I remember, fear overcame me and I could not understand what I was doing there. I felt real danger. Then out of nothing two girls started to hit my two close friends and they fought while everyone stood by to watch. I was expecting any minute to be jumped on in the same way as my friends. I remember just standing there watching. After about 10 minutes I suddenly looked behind me and I was surrounded solely by what looked like an army of only young men. There were about 40 or more in number. I thought "wow how strange, where did they all come from?" I also remember feeling a little embarrassed, being the only girl among them.

> *"...Do not fear, for those who are with us are more than those who are with them." And Elisha prayed and said, "Lord, I pray, open his eyes that he may see." Then the Lord opened the eyes of the young man, and he saw. And behold, the mountain was full of horses and chariots of fire all around Elisha.*
> *2 Kings 6:16-17*

Then I refocused on watching the fights. One of my closest friends was really receiving a beating, so I thought I might help her and break up the fight. But her opponent simply pushed me away in anger. So I walked away from the whole thing. I left with not one single hair on my head being touched and went home to my family. I remember wondering why the girl who wanted to beat me up, did not touch me. The next day, I saw my two friends with cuts and bruises on their faces. They looked subdued. I did not say a word. Anyway, it was Jasper, without me even asking, who explained to me in our conversation, the reason why I was not harmed in that incident. She said the boys told her this: "we told those girls, if anyone lays a hand on Tope; we are going to jump in to defend her." It then made sense to me why the boys surrounded me and why when I tried to stop the fight none of the older girls on the opponent's side saw that as an opportunity to attack me. To this day I am dumbfounded as to why the guys chose to protect me and not the other two. I can only look to God who is my helper in every time of need.

> *A thousand may fall at your side,*
> *and ten thousand at your right*
> *hand; but it shall not come near you.*
> *Only with your eyes shall you look,*
> *and see the reward of the wicked.*
> *Psalm 91:7-8*

I am not suggesting my two close friends were wicked as only God knows their hearts but I do know God's angels surrounded me in an obvious way, which caused me to look up again. Are you in the midst of a fight right now? Do you feel enough is enough and you just want peace but the opponent will not back off? Whether this be in the natural or in the spiritual; the Lord wants you to not fear but open your eyes and see the angels He has surrounding you. The Lord has gone before you and will fight for you.

About a month after speaking to Jasper, I remember my father saying to me, "it's about time you returned to church." I could not have agreed more. So I returned to our then local church, St Mary's, Church of England. Very soon after this I had some bible study sessions with the local vicar and my confirmation ceremony followed soon after. I remember saying the words of committing my life to Jesus at 16 years of age, knowing God and Jesus existed but not knowing why Jesus is God. My questions were not satisfactorily answered during bible studies. I asked "but how is Jesus the same as God?" the reply I received was, "He is, so take my word for it." That shut me up. The consequence of not having the gospel explained in more detail meant that I said the words of confirmation with head knowledge. My declaration of faith was not from the heart at that time. The heart is precious and really matters. God always looks at the heart and not the outer-man. Nevertheless, although there were still many unanswered questions lingering in my heart, I have never missed a Sunday of going to my 'home' church ever since. I will mention more about 'religion' in later chapters. But you see, like Joseph, I had to be *found* wandering, before I could see for myself I was wandering, lost in the wilderness.

Peter experienced a similar wavering when he was unsure if Jesus was who He claimed to be. Unbelief set in his heart as he began to doubt Jesus and even his own sanity. He did not want to be different from the crowd at large. He did not want to be singled out to be part of the perceived 'weak side', along with Jesus. As Jesus was being mocked, I suspect Peter felt mocked too. He was used to seeing miraculous signs and wonders by Jesus and everyone standing in awe and amazement. "Surely I must be dreaming, surely this can't be happening," he probably thought while he watched Jesus being questioned, spat on and physically abused by the religious leaders. There must have been an inner struggle. The feeling of being perhaps led astray, a feeling of wanting to be with Jesus, even if He was not who He claimed to be, Peter should have at least stood by Him as His close friend. Was Jesus of Nazareth not worth the loyalty of a friend? Peter may have been angry with Jesus inside for not allowing His disciple to defend Him physically. Peter's pride could have been dented when Jesus healed the ear of the soldier, he had heroically cut off with his sword. What was happening? What is this sign of weakness? Did not the Messiah come to save us? During Peter's 'wandering wilderness' experience, he would have certainly remembered the words of our Lord Jesus when He said:

> *"Take My yoke upon you and learn from Me, for I am gentle and lowly in heart, and you will find rest for your souls."*
> *Matthew 11:29*

Peter wept bitterly as flashbacks of our Lord's words would have come back to his mind. He saw signs & wonders, he watched miracles performed by the one he called master and teacher. How then was it so easy to deny Jesus when trials came? How easy is it for us to go our own way when we need to protect our reputation or simply fit into a crowd of people, we should not even be moving around with in the first place. Again, it always goes back to the condition of the heart.

In 2007, the Lord spoke to me in a dream and said, **"The condition of your heart, will determine your destiny."** I told this to my women's cell group and led several months of teaching about the issues of the heart. It was very effective as the Holy Spirit ministered to each one accordingly.

The reason why we wander is because God is dealing with our heart. Why do you think the Psalmist, David wrote:

> *'Search me, O God, and know my heart;*
> *try me, and know my anxieties; and*
> *see if there is any wicked way in me,*
> *and lead me in the way everlasting.*
> *Psalm 139:23-24*

These words followed an experience of David's as he wondered if we could ever hide from God after a realisation that this is impossible. God knit us together and our days have been ordained for us before even one of them came to be. When we try to hide from God and go our own way, we feel lost inside, just like Jonah. We need desperately to be shown His ways again. God's way is the only perfect way. The only way we will not stumble.

> *And you shall remember that the*
> *Lord Your God led you all the way*
> *these forty years in the wilderness,*
> *to humble you and test you, to know*
> *what was in your heart, whether you*
> *would keep His commandments or not.*
> *Deuteronomy 8:2*

Joseph too was struggling within himself as he was being tested. He half obeyed his father by going out to find his brothers. I can picture him deep down dragging his feet, getting lost along the way, with his head down.

Kicking the stones in the soil, observing cattle belonging to others. He may have been thinking about his dream and wishing it to come true quickly. He may have been hoping to find his brothers getting up to mischief, so he could gladly bring a bad report about them back to his father. As a man thinks, so he is. Joseph may have forgotten that his dreams came from the very heart of God and therefore were sacred. Not to be misused, or used for boasting. Dreams and visions from God are a form of signs and wonders (the prophetic). We must not play with them or treat them lightly. Joseph had to first be shown the condition of his heart before God could begin a work on his character.

'Now a certain man found him...' (Genesis 37:15a). When we are wandering, we need to be found by someone. Someone else has to do or say something for us to open our eyes and see the reality of our lives and ultimately the condition of our heart. When we drive a car, although there are side mirrors and one inside the car, there will always be grey areas we cannot see. These are called 'blind spots'. Bikers on the road are normally hit by vehicles they could not see due to the blind spots. It takes a loving person to show us, or at least we ought to be shown in love.

I believe God's first work on Joseph's character was to teach him how to fear the Lord.

> *The fear of the Lord is*
> *the beginning of wisdom.*
> *Proverbs 9:10*

Once we all learn to fear God, our heart is then opened for more fine-tuning. I believe the second work of Joseph's character was *humility*. This comes from having a *true* servant heart. When we learn to serve others, we learn what it is to put others first. We learn what it is like to become meek and lowly like Jesus. If we do not humble ourselves, when God's victories are seen through us, we would proudly and wrongly take all the glory. God quite clearly states that He will share His glory with no other.

> *Let nothing be done through selfish*
> *ambition or conceit, but in lowliness*
> *of mind let each esteem others better*
> *than himself. Let each of you look out*
> *not only for his own interests, but*
> *also for the interests of others. Let*
> *this mind be in you which was also in*
> *Christ Jesus, who, being in the form*
> *of God, did not consider it robbery to*
> *be equal with God, but made Himself*
> *of no reputation, taking the form of*

> *a bondservant, and coming in the*
> *likeness of men. And being found in*
> *appearance as a man, he humbled*
> *Himself and became obedient to*
> *the point of death of the cross.*
> *Philippians 2:3-8*

The Lord has recently put me in a church where I can learn true humility. A lifeboat church, where there is an outward focus. Bringing church to the unchurched; I am serving the poor and homeless in a community where there are many needing food and shelter. The beautiful thing about serving in this way is no one there has to know my status in society. We humble ourselves by making ourselves of no reputation and getting close to a people who are outcasts in society. When breakfast is being served to the hungry, it is about denying myself so they have more than enough, knowing that for most, that will be their only meal for that day and for some maybe for a few days. I am learning sacrificial living. God is doing a powerful work in my heart and shaping my character. I am on a journey with Him.

※ ※ ※

Chapter 6

❧ Dear Lord, who am I? ❦

...........And the man asked him,
saying, "What are you seeking?"
So he said, "I am seeking my
brothers. Please tell me where
they are feeding their flocks?"
Genesis 37:15b-16

After we have been found wandering, we pause and take a step back in order to re-evaluate our lives; we tend to look for things or people to fill the void in our hearts. God has put eternity on the hearts of all mankind, except we often first go our own way in finding eternity (Ecclesiastes 3:11). The study of psychology, they say, always leaves unanswered questions about why we human beings behave the way we do. Philosophers, Professors, Psychologists and Scientist become frustrated when in their own strength they are unable to unravel the truth about how fearfully and wonderfully we are made. The truth is, we are all seeking something.

> *And you will seek Me and find Me when*
> *you search for Me with all your heart.*
> *Jeremiah 29:13*

Most people have turned to smoking, drinking, drugs and rock & roll; some gambling, others pornography and sexual perversions; some false religion, especially delving into new age and the occult. I personally in the past have looked to my career, money (including get rich quick schemes), fashion, men and comfort eating. These are false gods. Who knows if Joseph became obsessed with his dreams? He may have made his dreams false gods to fill the void.

Sometimes we do not always find the One and only God when we look. But looking for something and seeking are two completely different things. Those of us who are parents will know the difference between when your child is looking for one of his/her school socks and after 30 seconds they tell you they cannot find it. In their half-hearted attempt to find their school sock they failed to look perhaps under the bed or underneath where they last saw it. Then you go and search for it, as it is the only clean one, since you have not done the

washing for a few days and bingo – you find it more
or less immediately. However, if your child had to find
his/her favourite toy, they would indeed search and not
give up so quickly. In fact, you might see a few tears of
frustration and in some cases grief.

Easter 2000, I went on a pilgrimage to the Holy
Land. This was always something I had wanted to do,
since my confirmation and to me meant getting closer
to God. Although I had been attending a church, I had
no personal relationship with Jesus. I still had many
unanswered questions including the one of why or how
is Jesus Christ the same as God. One could say I was
religious, in that I knew the 10 commandments; the
difference between right from wrong, I believed there
was a God and that Jesus died for our sins. But I had
never made Jesus Christ Lord of my life. I was still very
much in control of what I did and consulted nobody.

I remember around January or February 2000,
feeling a deep longing to draw near to Jesus, the
One whose image I had seen in the sky as a child. I
desperately wanted to also know my own identity and
the two seemed to go hand in hand without me actually
understanding why. I had separated from my former
husband about 3 months prior to these feelings and as
the hurt was still quite fresh, I felt as though I had lost

my identity. I was confused as to whether I was Mrs, Ms or Miss. I did not want my former partner's name but neither did I want to revert to my maiden name, which I had not had for 10 years and only reminded me of dysfunction. I felt very lost and vulnerable. I felt I did not fit anywhere. I did not fit in with the 'married' nor did I fit with the 'singles'. The trip to Israel was amazing in itself and I could write another book on this, but the point I am trying to get to is where we find our identity.

During this wonderful trip, I formed a close relationship with a dear English Christian woman. She took a liking to me as though I was her daughter. Everybody in my group were middle aged to elderly. Many were from middle-class, professional families. The other pilgrims knew I was an Accountant by profession and my newly found friend whom I called 'mum' on the trip was from Yorkshire. One evening about four of the other women were having a small get together in one of their rooms, which included snacks and wine. One of them invited me along but said it is by invite only, so I must not tell my friend. I felt a little uncomfortable about it as I wondered why they would leave anyone out. Anyway, I went along to this mini gathering and ate and drank and was quite happy to begin with, when one of them mentioned, how nice it was that professionals can get together like this. I looked surprised and another said to me "this party is only for the elite." They went on to mention how my friend who was a funeral director with a Northern accent and some of the others would not fit in to that gathering. I was horrified and saddened at the same time. I thought, "but are we not supposed to be Christians?" I quickly sipped a bit of my drink and said quietly that I better get off to bed and left feeling very sad. My friend was lovely and I could not imagine for a moment that people on this sort of trip would collude to single people out. I could see when I returned to my room that my friend knew the reason why she was not invited and I felt embarrassed for going. Obviously I was too naïve to see this beforehand. I thought what a messed up world we live in, here I am a black woman being included to a party full of white women who exclude white people from their inner circles if they are not considered the elite. I did not get it. Conditional acceptance is wrong. We all may have made errors like this in our lives. If so, it is good to repent.

When we put ourselves or other people in boxes and attach labels, we form ungodly beliefs, which reign over our minds and can form strongholds. It can also lead to the alienation of a different label.

There are positive labels and negative labels, both can be as harmful as the other. For instance, 'White Men can't Jump' or "Why Should White Guys Have All the Fun?" are titles of well-known entertainment; a film and a book respectively. On one end of the spectrum, white men could go away with the negative belief that they really cannot jump as high as black or Hispanic men and feel inferior in their physical capabilities. Therefore, if white boys/men accept this label, they may not even try to jump. 'Jump' can mean so many things. Jumping is a form of leaping towards something high and scoring. It does something to a man's ego when they score and everyone who sees or hears of it cheers and perceives them as successes or heroes. On the other hand, having 'fun' is what all men want to have both in and out of the work place. The book "Why Should White Guys Have All the Fun?" was written in order to debate why there appear to be more successful white professional/business men than there are black or men from another ethnicity. The sad thing is, whether it is true or not, non-white men, if they believe this, may feel like it is not worth even trying to become successful in business or professionally. And those who do attempt it may experience fear and low self-esteem along the way, whilst their counterparts may feel superior in the workplace in order to compensate for their negative labels.

Nevertheless, both extremes are ungodly beliefs because the truth is, we can do all things through Christ who strengthens us (Philippians 4:13).

Today, many of the youth are in gangs for the purpose of identity. Even if it means taking innocent lives, simply to feel they belong. We live in a generation where there is a love deficit, as more families fall apart, and where families are intact; there is a growing absenteeism of true parenthood on the rise. Both parents may be there in the physical but are not supportive spiritually, emotionally or mentally for their children. In some households there is only abuse in the exact areas where support is required. Many adults today walk around in self-hatred. Some feel like failures, where they have not lived up to the expectations of others or their own. If you do not love yourself, it is impossible to love others. Most fathers project this self-hatred onto their own children without even realising it. Children grow up apart from their parents due to the pain they suffer under such parenthood. All they want is love, acceptance and understanding. If they cannot get this from within the home, they will go elsewhere to find it. The saddest thing is many households, including the middleclass have a big elephant in their home but cannot see it. They would rather blame it on someone else in society or live in complete denial. As a result, young adults are given labels by society, which add salt to the wound. Drugs are infiltrating the young generation but the pushers report to the invisible rich and wicked at the top of the game. These hidden criminals do everything possible to disguise their identity in order to maintain a false reputation in society. However, we must not forget the source of all wickedness is Satan. The devil wants to shred the family to pieces as his intention was by uprooting Joseph from his. But God in His infinite wisdom has a plan.

Joseph was obviously put in a box and labelled. His category did not fit with the type of his brothers. He was the second youngest of his brothers with no mother to 'mother' him. He may have received sympathy from his brother's mothers and the occasional patronising. He may have been intentionally excluded from some social events or gatherings. He may have grown tired of the labels, so at the first opportunity of discovering who he really was through his dream, he may not have been able to help but blurt it out. God uses the weak and what people perceive as foolish to confound the wise. Young David, the one they sidelined, unlike Joseph, who although he knew he was anointed to be king of Israel, did not speak this out among his older brothers. It appeared David lost his mother at an early age too. But he seemed more secure in his youth than Joseph. I believe his relationship with God was closer than Joseph in his youth. Hence, why God said "David is a man after My own heart." Joseph however could not contain himself. He may have formed an ungodly belief about himself and needed to break free from that mindset and the lies of the enemy. Only God can set us free from captivity. We must not seek false gods to fill the void in our hearts. We must seek and trust God, our source.

We must repent if we have gone seeking false gods to fill the gaps.

Then Paul stood in the midst of the Areopagus and said, "Men of Athens, I perceive that in all things you are very religious; for as I was passing through and considering the objects of your worship, I even found an altar with this inscription:

TO THE UNKNOWN GOD

> *Therefore, the One who you worship without knowing, Him I proclaim to you: God who made the world and everything in it, since He is Lord of heaven and earth, does not dwell in temples made with hands. Nor is He worshipped with men's hands, as though He needed anything, since He gives all life, breath, and all things. And He has made from one blood every nation of men to dwell on all the*

> *face of the earth, and has determined
> their preappointed times and the
> boundaries of their dwellings, so that
> they should seek the Lord, in the hope
> that they might grope for Him and find
> Him, though He is not far from each
> one of us; for in Him we live and move
> and have our being, as also some of
> your own poets have said, 'For we are
> also His offspring.' Therefore, since
> we are the offspring of God, we ought
> not to think that the Divine Nature is
> like gold or silver or stone, something
> shaped by art and man's devising.
> Truly, these times of ignorance God
> overlooked, but now commands
> all men everywhere to repent..."*
> *Acts 17:22-30*

During my Israel trip we visited a beautiful church building used by the Catholics. The paintings all around the walls and ceiling told a pictorial story of Jesus' birth to his death and resurrection. I was in awe of God at this point coupled with all the other places we had just visited. I was still hiding behind false identity and labels at this time. Desperate to know who I am. So I got on my knees to pray. My prayer was simply this: Dear Lord, who am I? I remained still in His presence and all of a sudden I heard a voice say, **"You are who you are."**

"You are who you are." I quickly opened my eyes in total shock and looked to my left and right expecting to see someone or thought maybe others heard it too, but there was no one near me and everyone else seemed to be minding their own business. I quickly closed my eyes again and smiled after realising, I just heard the voice of God. I said thank You Lord and then stood up, went outside and it seemed as though the air was different. I sat down to reflect on His words and as I pondered this famous scripture came to mind:

"I AM WHO I AM."
Exodus 3:14

Then the penny dropped and I was free. I felt so light inside. The Lord was telling me that my identity is not found in my status, title, colour, class, race, qualifications, family name, who I knew or did not know or anything else for that matter. But my identity is found in Christ who is the Great I Am. We are made in God's image according to His likeness, so if He is who He is, then we are who we are; unique in every way. It is important we know who we are in Christ. There are some scriptures at the back of this book to encourage you in this.

Those who put people in a box also tend to put God in a box. They limit God, saying "surely God cannot talk to us today? Surely that was only for those days. After all we have the bible now." I feel so sad when I hear this. God is omnipotent, omnipresent and omniscient. There is none like Him and He is the same yesterday, today and forever. Dreams and visions are still here today for our tomorrow. As we go through our journey we need to use our spiritual gifts for the common good. Those who limit God also limit their ministry. Not that they are not saved but they may have a tendency not to allow the Holy Spirit to move in the direction He wants to. There are many ministries today built on human strength, which lack joy. We do indeed hear from God through His written word and also His rhema word. He has left His Holy Spirit with us in order to use our gifts for such a time as this.

> *Jesus said:* **"...and greater works than these he will do..."**
> *John 14:12.*

Although I was set free at that time, I have to ensure that I remain in complete freedom, because the enemy will always try to use people who are insecure around us to sow ungodly seeds in our hearts and put us back in a box with a label and the lid tightly fixed on. Some will use words which make us feel as though we amount to nothing, or will continuously compare us with others or themselves, as though God made a mistake in making us. People may tell you, you cannot do certain things until you are healed or until, they say so. This is to make them feel powerful and to make you feel weak. It amounts to control. This may be a trap of the enemy to prevent us from moving forward and stepping out into what God has for us. Hurt can arise as a result. Unforgiveness can manifest in our hearts. Ungodly beliefs are often very subtle. You do not know they are there unless it is pointed out to you. This is exactly what happened to me this year. I did not realise I was partly paralysed by an ungodly belief I carried around for about 3 years. Lies from the enemy were trying to hold me back and cause me to stagnate. I thank God for His ministry through the Catch the Fire Toronto team who visited London in August 2009. I have been completely set free from an ungodly belief and now I walk in victory into what God has called me to do – Kingdom business.

Do you want to be set free from ungodly beliefs? Do you want to jump out of that box with labels attached and walk into what God has for you? Then replace the lie with truth. Ask Him to give you a word which replaces the lies. It may not make sense at first. For instance, when I went through this prayer myself, during ministry time, the Lord gave me the word 'Safe'. As I heard it again and again, I became frustrated because I was expecting a word, which is opposite to the lies the devil had sown inside me. I thought the word safe was irrelevant and dismissed it at first. But the minister helped me to open up the word and see what the Lord was saying to me. She said, "could the Lord be saying: 'It is SAFE for you to step out into what He has for you?' " At hearing this I felt the power of the Holy Spirit inside of me and the fire of revival was set ablaze within the pit of my stomach, which felt hot. Then the fire spread all over my body. Eventually, something broke and the liberty from within me caused me to laugh and laugh at the thought of even believing the lie of the enemy in the first place. The battlefield is indeed in the mind. But one thing I know for a fact, The Holy Spirit has a good sense of humour. He turns our sorrow into dancing. He loves to set the prisoners free. The devil hates it when God's children walk in freedom. The devil uses that unclean Jezebel spirit to control God's people, so they will not do what they have been called to do. What is the point of living if you are not living for your purpose?

Whilst on the floor, drunk on the Holy Sprit, this scripture then came into my spirit:

The name of the Lord is a strong tower;
the righteous run to it and are safe.
                              Proverbs 18:10

The enemy was trying to put the brakes on me moving forward into my destiny. When you are not living for purpose, you are stuck or in stagnation. You walk around as if your heart is sick because you are not being who you are. You find you may be trying to be who you are not, simply because someone else has put you in a box with labels and expects you to perform to their standards or beliefs. But when the Holy Spirit comes and sets you free, your heart is no longer sick but full of hope and joy. I have since forgiven those people who the enemy used to sow the seed of ungodly belief and moved on. You are who you are. Live for purpose my friends; live for purpose.

At this stage, I believe it is important for me to be truthful concerning the area of unforgiveness. Although I spoke words of forgiveness for a particular person who kept hurting me whenever I became vulnerable, I realised a couple of weeks later, I had not truly forgiven this person. The hurts still repeated on me whenever I thought of the incidents that affected me so deeply. Then one day a couple of months after the immersion weekend, I sat in my church, St Andrew's and listened

to the Minister preaching on the Fruit of the Spirit –
Patience. She said one sentence and this is what released
me into full genuine forgiveness. The Minister said,
"Patience is an ingredient for forgiveness." It was after
hearing this and before I took Holy Communion, I was
filled with compassion and chose to let go completely
and repented for holding on. I then took communion
and healing tears streamed down my face as I felt the
Holy Angels ministering to me. At that point, I felt closer
to God and so much lighter. I knew I could eat and drink
with and even hug this person again, if it came to that.
In fact I called to tell them how much I love them when
I arrived home. I knew deep down they still needed a lot
of healing due to damage caused by the past and I need
only to be patient because God is Jehovah Raphah; the
God who heals.

Who am I?

Can words ever explain?
Isn't who I am plain?
What do you see?
What do you see in me?
I am a created being
Came without me knowing,
Grew without me sowing
Ordained from the beginning,
I am my hiding place

I am full of grace,
I am lost but found
I am one of a kind,
I am unique full of potion
I am something in motion,
I am lost in wonder
I am always growing fonder,
I am but a breeze
I am sometimes a tease,
I am here today gone tomorrow
I am someone people borrow,
I am not what you want me to be
I am not you and you are not me,
I am not Mary, Jack or Ilene
Nor am I Saul, Beth or Catherine,
In fact I don't know who you are Sam?
But Someone once told me – I am who I am.

By Tope Teniola 30/06/10
© Copy Right 2010

❋ ❋ ❋

Chapter 7

❧ There are Angels in the Pit ❧

Then they said to one another, "Look, this dreamer is coming! Come, therefore, let us now kill him and cast him into some pit; and we shall say some wild beast has devoured him. We shall see what will become of his dreams!"

Genesis 37:19-20

Joseph, although he needed a lot of work on his character, I doubt would ever have dreamt of killing anybody. Do you know how precious our lives here on earth are? What right does anyone have to physically damage or kill a person? Even to confess physically harming someone with your mouth is just as effective as actually doing it, especially when it is spoken to the person you feel like harming. If you say you have made

Jesus the Lord of your life and still breathe violence, then something is fundamentally wrong because the two do not mix.

> *For out of the abundance of*
> *the heart, the mouth speaks.*
> *Matthew 12:34*

One would have thought Joseph said to his brothers "I had a dream that you were all beaten up by me" that would have caused them to want to kill him. And even then, nothing justifies hurting someone and taking their life. If you do not see eye to eye with someone or that person is making you feel hurt or causing strife between you, it's better if you part from that person, so you all live your lives in peace. This is what Abraham did with his nephew, Lot. He could see strife building up as they kept having dispute after dispute. Wisdom and love told Abraham to separate from Lot. Abraham walked with God and his faith allowed it. Abraham knew God had a plan for his life and did not want to waste time in petty arguments that did not glorify God.

> *As far as it depends on you do your*
> *best to live in peace with your brother.*
> *Romans 12:18.*

How then did Joseph's older brothers who were born from the same father, become murderers? You may argue they had different mothers. Cain and Abel were from the same mother and father (Adam & Eve) but still one was a murderer. The answer therefore, always goes back to the condition of one's heart. It has nothing to do with mother, father, race, gender, external beauty or ugliness but the heart. Joseph's brothers had no relationship with God. They did not love God at this stage of their lives, as we cannot say we love God but hate our brother (1 John 4:20).

> *For this is the message that you heard from the beginning, that we should love one another, not as Cain who was of the wicked one and murdered his brother. And why did he murder him? Because his works were evil and his brother's righteous. Do not marvel, my brethren, if the world hates you.*
> *1 John 3:13*

I personally believe Joseph sensed his brothers hated him. Those who have the gift of the prophetic will easily pick up on these things. But he had no bible to show him that they could potentially kill him like Cain did his brother. Even David had to be warned by King Saul's daughter to flee for his life, because his heart was pure.

Thank God we have the bible today. Joseph, who was in his teens, only knew not to be around his brothers voluntarily because he felt excluded. Joseph still loved his brothers, as they were family. As we know he was sent by Israel, his father to look for his brothers and he eventually obeyed. He did not go voluntarily.

When a person is consumed with hate, this is nothing to be taken lightly. Even in the churches, some leaders play down hatred as though it would just go away by itself. Most of the time we find that those people who hate others, also hate themselves. Self-hatred is a dangerous demon. Suicidal thoughts are born out of self-hatred. The spirit of death lurks around self-hatred. The source of hatred is Satan; he hates God and His children. But he needs a physical body to use to attack God's children. I call it 'spirit children cleansing'. When there is strife in a church, it means some people have opened the door to the enemy because instead of fixing their eyes on Jesus, they were busy looking at others in the church. Sometimes when a person hates another intensely but is unable to express it openly due to their position, they would rather turn a blind eye when someone else is hurting and they know they could do something about it. They can even go as far as to rub salt into the wound by turning one against another by using the other person, who also hates that person against them in subtle ways. We have all heard of 'contract killings'. Well, this can be done through a person in a spiritual setting. Where a person tries to crush the soul and quench the spirit of another in church. So although the natural body has not been killed, a person uses subtle words or actions against another like a dripping tap, long enough to lead to the other person feeling crushed and spiritually 'good for nothing'. But God does not sleep. Whatever is done in darkness will be brought into the light. God will always deliver a righteous person out of the hands of Satan.

> *Whoever hates his brother is a murderer and you know that no murderer has eternal life abiding in him.*
> *1 John 3:15*

In any type of family setting, where hatred is discerned, the elders must intercede for the children/flock. Sensitivity is crucial and it is also important not to take sides. Genuine love and forgiveness must be encouraged and gossip and murmuring must be quenched. It is not of God to force two individuals to be reconciled, as this must only come through the guidance of the Holy Spirit. Prayer is more powerful, so individuals do not feel coerced or that there is a bias. There is nothing impossible for God. Individuals will be convicted as we allow God's word to dwell richly in our hearts. When forgiveness is genuine on both sides, there is a peace, which calms the storm, and one is able to move on. When there is no forgiveness, even from one side, you will find that one individual finds it difficult to let go of the other. He/She will always feel that the other individual owes him/her something. If this is you today, I have three words for you, 'LET IT GO!'

Jesus emphasised uncleanliness comes from within a man and has nothing to do with what a man eats (Mark 7:14-23). Evil words and deeds begin with evil thoughts, which are birthed in the heart. There is a well-known saying, "You can't prevent a bird from flying over your head, but you can stop it from building a nest in your hair." Birds build their nest stick by stick, so are evil thoughts built in a similar way. Also birds of the same feather flock together. When there is hurt in an immature Christian, he or she may try hard to drag others into their circle to form pity parties. They huddle together sometimes without realising they have given the devil a foothold. Above all else, we must guard our hearts – the heart is wicked and deceitful beyond cure, who can understand it? (Jeremiah 17:9). Hence, why all

Christians should remain accountable to one another, especially when we are in ministry.

Bitterness

When the root is bitter
The tree leaves start to wither,
Though it's dark, it seems there is no light
When the air is grim and bulbs catch sight?
When will the blossoms sprout?
When will the branch stop shaking?
It seems scared –
Like a frightened child,
Life is too much to handle,
Much love needed
But not reciprocated
It shouts I need water!
Feed me, feed me now!
Will not the Lord ever prune me?
It's not fair –
I want to bear fruit like all the others.

Proverbs 7:9

© By Tope Teniola 21/05/05

The root of anger, hatred, bitterness and murder usually comes from jealousy or unforgiveness.

When I was a college student at 17 years of age, I had a Saturday job, working for Aramis in Selfridges, London. I was dating a very handsome young man of 21 years who was also a full time university student. He was a popular man among the women. In fact most women approached him, rather than the other way around. My father did not let me out of the home much and I certainly could not stay out till late at night. As mentioned before, I did not allow my then boyfriends to go all the way, so eventually they would look elsewhere. One day at home, I received a telephone call from an anonymous woman. She said she was calling on behalf of her friend, who was dating my boyfriend. I asked her how she got my telephone number but she did not reply. She said his friends told her friend that I was his girlfriend and she was finding out if this was true. She said her friend is dating him. She was very forceful and abrupt. Then when I confessed I was, she started to threaten me. She said, "We know where you live and you will be followed, if you don't keep away from him, we will kill you." Her voice was so intense and filled with anger & emotion. I was very scared and said to her "it sounds like you are not calling on behalf of your friend but for yourself." She then hung up on me.

I did not tell my father because he did not agree with me having boyfriends in the first place and I had no mother to confide in. I then thought I could turn to my then boyfriend, whom I called and he not only denied it, he was rude to me and was not supportive at all, so our relationship was ended. I was totally on my own in this. I went to bed scared and woke up Saturday morning fearful. I travelled to work terrified and by the time I got to Selfridges, my face probably looked like I had seen a ghost. I felt empty inside, my body was stiff and I felt in despair with no one to talk to. There were 2 of us serving on the counter that day and we took it in turns to go on our breaks. When my colleague went for her lunch first, I clambered up in the corner of my counter, expecting my unknown enemies to pounce on me. Thinking to myself, how I might die, what weapon they may use, would it be a knife or a gun or would they just beat me until my heart stopped. Thoughts like these filled my mind and I became completely deflated, I simply wanted go home and cry buckets. There were a lot of customers in the store itself but thankfully, I thought, no one for a long time had come to my counter to enquire of the products. As I cowered in a standing up/sitting down position at the corner of the counter, an unusual man came walking towards me. The reason why I say unusual was because as I was daydreaming and staring at the floor, I first saw his feet appear. He wore brown leather sandals in autumn time, grey trousers and an Ibadan style short sleeve top (similar to what Nigerian men wear as one of their national costume). He was a slightly tanned Caucasian man, with black hair and a beard.

Now, if you can imagine all this happening simultaneously as I saw him, my body was drawn toward him like a magnet. I stood straight and walked straight over to him and my body was pressed on the counter as though ready to serve him. There was silence as I stood there staring at him in wonder. In my spirit, I sensed this man was holy. I had never seen him before but I felt extremely safe near him and felt a heavenly presence. I was stunned at this sudden change of atmosphere.

Now the first thing I said sounds very peculiar to this day. Instead of saying hello, how may I be of assistance? I asked him something I have never asked a customer in my life, "Where are you from?" My tone was gentle and I was in awe. He answered, "Brazil, where are you from?" I was surprised he was interested in something so irrelevant at such a time as this, I replied as though it did not really matter, "oh Nigeria." He then held out his hand for me to spray it with some cologne. I was horrified to think a man so holy should not try what became apparent to me for the first time, something so unholy. Nobody had told me cologne was unclean but at that particular time I became aware of it in my spirit. Then I reluctantly sprayed the back of his hand and he smelt it. I could feel inside of me, I wanted to ask so many questions about life and about why I am here. The burning questions I would have asked Jesus, had I been alive during the time He walked on earth in the flesh. In fact I did not want this man to leave my presence but I was in a sort of trance I could not think where to begin. He smiled as though he knew my thoughts and slowly walked away. I remained in this trance for about 30 seconds thereafter. Then suddenly a surge of joy, peace, love and courage filled my heart. So much I leapt from my counter to see if I could see him again but he was nowhere in sight. I thought to myself, how could he have possibly disappeared so fast for someone who drifted as he walked. I looked left and right in excitement and almost forgot I was meant to be working. My stature was straight I was full of boldness.

When my colleague returned from her lunch break, she looked surprised at the transformation in me as my eyes lit up and I could not stop talking to her with great enthusiasm, laughter and encouragement. I literally skipped into the lift with a broad smile as I spoke friendly to the customers on my way up to the cafeteria. Somehow, I knew the Lord has visited me and I did not know it. I was completely healed and delivered from fear and had faith that God was with me. I have never looked over my shoulder since that time. I truly believe the Lord sent His angel in my time of desperate need, not only to watch over me but also to remind me that He is and will always watch over and protect me. To this day, I confirm my testimony to be true and not exaggerated. I testify that God is real, living, active and love. Every testimony of mine in this book is for His glory alone.

> *Surely the Lord is in this place*
> *and I was not aware of it.*
> *Genesis 28:16*

Have you ever felt like rubbish or garbage? Have you ever been threatened or treated so disrespectfully, it was as if your life did not matter to those people? Have you ever been in a situation where people would rather see you dead than alive due to the intense hatred in their heart? Joseph was thrown away like a piece of junk. That is what hatred coupled with anger in one's heart does. No value is placed on the hated individual. Joseph's brothers did not know back then, that like they were, Joseph also was fearfully and wonderfully made by the Most High God in His image, according to His likeness. When we dishonour our brother or neighbour in this way, we dishonour God.

Rejection comes in many different forms and for many different reasons. The rejecter is usually the one who is hurting in some way to cause them to reject others. Sometimes a person feels they need to reject someone for their own protection based on reasoning. However, there are times when there is no rationale behind the rejection. Nevertheless, rejection is hurtful and can be ugly.

When I announced the man I was to marry, to my father, he became so angry, he wrote me a long letter stating quite clearly that I was no longer his daughter. He disowned me and this intensified the loss of my mother. I was 22 years old at the time and had no real understanding of life. I became more vulnerable than I already was and felt as though I was an orphan. I felt like abandoning the man I fell in love with in university and running back to my father. But I did not. I cried and lost my appetite for several days. I sat wondering if my father ever loved me or was I a possession to him. After all, I had not committed a crime; I only just wanted to be happy and wanted my father's blessing. I would liken this feeling to being in the pit. I was in this pit of rejection for 10 years. This was the length of time my father and I did not speak to each other. This was a dry time for me. I graduated, got married, gave birth to a child, was invited to sit in prestigious positions in business and third sector, but something was missing. I realised after my marriage had ended, I was fearful of my father and had held unforgiveness towards him for many years. I had therefore dishonoured my father and the bible speaks clearly about this. Although my father had rejected me, it was because he was hurt I was going against his wishes. I failed in those 10 years to be grateful and show compassion towards my father. I thank God; I am no longer in this pit. After separating from my husband in 1999, I wrote a humble letter of gratitude and apology to my father. I really could not bear the thought of my father dying before I could tell him how much I loved him. We were reconciled in January 2000. He said our reunion felt like he had just won the Pools. This was the first time he had met my son who was 6 years old then. This is an example of the damage rejection causes.

I have been rejected by Nigerian people for not being Nigerian enough. I do not speak the language or have the accent and so do not fit into their circles. Nor had I been to Nigeria back then, so was not familiar with their custom. I used to try hard to fit in to the extent I became culturally confused, so I stayed on the parameters and owned up to being simply British. I realise not only is it impossible to please everyone, it is too late to change things. So the famous saying comes to mind:

"God grant me the serenity to accept the things I cannot change, the courage to change the things I can, and the wisdom to know the difference."

A recent incident, which I find quite funny to this day, was when a Rasta man was walking ahead of me in the street. I was running a little late for a meeting, so had to move quickly. I walked briskly, and then jogged a little. As I jogged past, this man shouted, "what happen sister?" For a minute I was not sure if he was talking to me or someone else, nevertheless I continued in my hurry as I focused of getting to the meeting. Then I heard this same man shout in an angry voice, "What, you can't say hello and you call yourself a dread – go way!" I was stunned and then realised he must have been speaking to me. That was acceptance and rejection by a complete stranger within 30 seconds and I believe it should be noted in the Guinness Book of World Records.

The truth is, we have all been rejected at some stage of our lives. Remember the aim of the enemy is to make the person feel as though they do not fit. And when we have been rejected by a parental figure, this can give us a distorted picture of God. I strongly recommend the book called 'The Shack' by WM Paul Young. We may grow up subconsciously believing God is like man; hence have a distorted view of God. I used to think God only loved me conditionally, so when I messed up, I would be so hard on myself, to the point of depression, even though I had repented. I used to visualise myself crying, whilst clinging to my Daddy in heaven's legs, hanging onto him whilst He walked in case He tried to walk away from me and abandon me. I was terrified of the consequences after considering temptation. The result of constant rejection is unwholeness. Internally, I was shattered, even after giving my life to Jesus. The healing process can take years. This can be likened with the pit experience of Joseph. Let us put our feet in Joseph's shoes for a moment. One minute, he is relieved to see his brothers, the next minute, his coat of many colours is being torn off of him and he is being lifted off and thrown into a pit.

There was Joseph, in the pit, he now had no mother and was removed from his father. Overnight, Joseph became a homeless orphan. A teenager crushed inside and being pushed into the unknown. Joseph's mind would have been frazzled and fearful, not knowing whether he was going to live or die. He needed love and affection. He needed his father. Where was his father? How could his father not have seen this coming? Was Jacob too engaged with his other family affairs and business to realise Joseph needed quality time spent with him, love and affection more than material things?

Joseph's 'love language' may have been quality time and physical touch. Joseph may have been able to tell his father how he was really feeling inside about his brothers' behaviour towards him. Israel could have offered emotional support, protection and wisdom to the awkward situation. After all, Joseph was outnumbered.

Absent fathers are a growing problem in the World today. The God ordained 'family' forms the very fabric of society and that has sadly been shattered by pride, women's liberation, divorce, infidelity, addictions, debt and money worries, which are the biggest case of relationship breakdown and lead to housing and health and employment problems. God's heart is for the orphaned children. In fact His heart cries out for them. There are over 143 million orphans in the world today. However, these figures do not include the children who live with parents physically but mentally, emotionally and spiritually absent. Many men and women today go about life with orphan spirits, desperately looking for a replacement mother and father figure. We all need a covering. Christ is our covering as the Head of the Church. But not all people know Christ as our covering.

> *Then they took him and cast*
> *him into a pit. And the pit was*
> *empty; there was no water in it.*
> *Genesis 37:24*

When we are rejected it often feels like a place of dullness and dryness. We become outcast within seconds and often we do not necessarily understand why until much later. Joseph would have sensed evil when he was being thrown in the pit. In the pit of wilderness there is nothing but desert sand. It is also colourless. Joseph's identity and dignity was stripped from him. Without water or rescue, we die. Likewise, without the Word of God to rescue us from spiritual dryness, we die spiritually. I would say for me personally, between the age of 10 and 31, was the driest time of my life. The woman at the well had this same pit experience and Jesus saw it. Her life was being lived in the pit.

> *Jesus answered and said to her,* **"Whoever drinks of this water will thirst again, but whoever drinks of the water that I shall give him will never thirst. But the water that I shall give him will become in him a fountain of water springing up into everlasting life"** *The woman said to Him, "Sir, give me this water, that I may not thirst, nor come here to draw."*
> *John 4:13-15*

If that woman had died that same morning before her encounter with Jesus she would have gone to hell, as she was living in sin. Jesus was this woman's deliverer and eternal life giver. Had Jesus not saved her, the people in her village would have also perished. At the salvation of one ordinary but yet significant woman, a whole village was saved. Reuben and Judah acted symbolically as Christ and became Joseph's deliverer both from the pit and from death. Joseph at that time had no idea that the Lord had chosen them to save him from death. Neither did Reuben or Judah know that their good heart and deed would be written in history books. They simply realised the injustice in killing an innocent person and had found love deep down in their hearts for their younger brother and did not want to see bloodshed. Thank God their brothers listened to them. Judah said:

> *"Come let us sell him to the Ishmaelites, and let not our hand be upon him, for he is our brother and our flesh." And his brothers listened.*
> *Gen37: 27*

There were indeed angels in the pit with Joseph just like there were angels in the Den with Daniel. These are the angels who rescue us from death. Like the two I testified about earlier.

For He shall give His angels charge
over you. To keep you in all your ways.
Psalm 91:11

The empire of angels is as vast as God's creation and it is impossible to count them. Even though one-third fell from heaven to earth when Lucifer rebelled, the remainder, who are God's messengers, are innumerable. I have learnt angels do not marry, procreate or have sex and are created by God to do His will. They are to serve God in heaven and also release His will on earth.

'Are not all angels ministering
spirits sent to serve those
who will inherit salvation?'
Hebrews 1:14

All Christians are heirs of salvation, who are placed in Christ and now live in heavenly places. We have forgiveness of sins, the healing of our body and soul and deliverance from demons because of what Jesus did for us on the cross. He sends His angels to save and deliver us.

There are some angels who are called 'Living Creatures' in the bible. These angels join us in praise and worship. I once heard angels singing when I was in a church prayer meeting. We were praying in preparation for a service where the visiting preacher was to be Tony Hinn, Pastor Benny Hinn's brother. As about 30 of us sang in the upstairs hall, I heard a choir that sounded so harmonic and out of this world, I knew it could not be us. The choir seemed to be coming out from the brick walls so I looked over and saw only a few of the Christian men standing there. But the choir had a mixture of feminine voices. I thought this is strange but so beautiful; in fact, it was the most beautiful choir I had ever heard, I did not want it to stop. When I went downstairs very moved and in awe, I dared not to mention it to anyone in case they thought I was hearing things. As I stood at the entrance to welcome the guests and congregation coming into the main hall, one of the sisters asked me "did you hear the angels singing?" I was so excited I rejoiced with her knowing I was not the only one who heard. I asked some others who said they did not hear, so I realised maybe it was only meant for a few people to hear the sound of angels joining us in simple but heart felt praise and worship in a small prayer meeting.

These angels also rescue our identity and dignity by restoring us fully in Christ. All the things the enemy has stolen from us, these angels restore. I could say I lost my identity temporarily from receiving rejection from both Nigerians and English; from my former husband; from family; from friends; from colleagues; from church members and leaders. But thank God I no longer look for my identity in my race, nationality, colour, gender, religion, status, position or valuables but I have found my identity solely in Jesus Christ, my Rock and my Redeemer. I am only passing through this earth – my true citizenship is in heaven.

If you have not yet seen an angel, it is because you have not needed to see one. God knows what we need. Therefore, when you need to see an angel, you will – God will make sure of that.

Remember the devil has come to steal, kill and destroy. He seeks to remove our parental and spiritual covering and will stop at nothing to see society fall and delights when people blame God for his mess. I do not believe for a moment that Joseph thought the God of Abraham, Isaac and Jacob had forsaken him in the pit. When a true child of God receives rejection, although we may also receive an orphan spirit at the time, there is something inside of us, which I believe is the Holy Spirit who dwells within us, reassuring us, we are not orphans but heirs of God.

The Apostle Paul wrote:

> *For you did not receive the spirit of bondage again to fear, but you received the Spirit of adoption by whom we cry out, "Abba, Father." The Spirit Himself bears witness with our spirit that we are children of God, and if children, then heirs – heirs of God and joint heirs with Christ, if indeed we suffer with Him, that we may also be glorified together. For I consider that the sufferings of this present time are not worthy to be compared with the glory which shall be revealed in us. For the earnest expectation of the creation eagerly waits for the revealing of the sons of God.*
>
> *Romans 8:15-19*

❊ ❊ ❊

Chapter 8

The Authority within
❧ the Slave ❧

*Then Midianite traders passed by;
so the brothers pulled Joseph up and
lifted him out of the pit and sold him
to the Ismaelites for twenty shekels of
silver. And they took Joseph to Egypt.*

Genesis 37:28

Joseph, whilst being lifted out of the pit, may have
thought his brothers had repented or were joking about.
He would have been further shocked to see how serious
his brothers (except Reuben) were about getting him out
of their sight. Joseph was not only sold into bondage
but to foreigners, those who did not worship the God
of his father, grandfather and great grandfather, but
those who worshipped Idols. Joseph instantly became
a stranger with no sense of belonging; unknown to

his new masters and in the foreign land where he was transported to be a slave. What does slavery actually mean? Slave means: captive; person without freedom or personal rights; one dominated by another; one in bondage. Slavery is another form of rejection, that is, rejection of who God has called you to be and acceptance of what the slaver/slave owner wants you to be. Slavery is the enemy's way of trying to rob one's true identity.

God has given us all a free will and the devil hates this because he does not have the same free will we have. He was created an angel, who as I mentioned in an earlier chapter, was created to serve God and His servants (man). Angels are not made in the image or likeness of God. Their will is limited. If they rebel against God, they automatically choose to follow Satan's destiny in hell. Fallen angels are known as demons and require someone else's physical body to inhabit in order to operate their wickedness. Demons cannot change their will to do good, but the human being in which they dwell, through deliverance can. When a human being desires to do good, turn from evil and follow God, the deliverance process begins. Most people when deliverance has taken place often testify to feeling light weight. This is where the anointing of God has broken yokes and burdens. The shackles, which the demons used to bind up the person's will in whom they dwelled, are broken because that person is expecting God to free them from captivity.

Captivity for most is a dark place. The Lord, our Saviour brings us from darkness into His glorious light. We must not underestimate the power of darkness but neither must we underestimate the mighty power of God, who is LIGHT.

> *That was the true Light which gives light to every man coming into the world.*
> *John 1:9*

The mentality of a slaver or a slave owner is that of lust for money and power. I have never viewed a slave owner as powerful but weak and fearful inside. They have a deep need to feel superior and always in control. They have no compassion or feeling for another human neither do they care about another human's rights. They only care for themselves and focus on greedy intent. There is no light to be found within them.

> *For we do not wrestle against flesh and blood, but against principalities, against powers, against the rulers of the darkness of this age, against spiritual hosts of wickedness in the heavenly places.*
> *Ephesians 6:12*

To treat another human being who was made in the likeness of God, like a wild dog is to dishonour God. The bible says pride is an abomination to God. Slavery was birthed out of pride. The bible also says:

> *The love of money is the root of all kinds of evil.*
> *1 Timothy 6:10a*

So a slaver is driven by a lust for riches and is wicked without remorse. There have been many stories of barbaric treatment of slaves to the point of death. Some slaves have families, including little children who have to witness the derogatory and often cruel treatment of their loved ones, watching all their dignity disappear. When slavery and cruelty becomes acceptable in a society, there is something fundamentally wrong within the fabric of that community. The door has been open for evil in a colossal way and people either have been blinded or choose to turn a blind eye towards oppression and injustice. Some Christians, even today do not stand up to what is obviously evil in our society.

Even I have been guilty of seeing injustice or systemic evil and saying 'that has nothing to do with me.' Some injustices are extremely subtle or came about through negligence or neglect. For those people who are overwhelmed by debt and harassed by creditors or have gone to prison through non payment of certain priority debts or are bankrupt, or suicidal, they are in a form of bondage.

> "........the borrower is
> servant to the lender"
> Proverbs 22:7b

The devil's tactics are very subtle at times and we may not always see the spiritual effect of the culture of over spending and excessive borrowing, which is so rife in the Western world, including the churches.

> "And the creditor is
> coming to take my two
> sons to be his slaves."
> 2 Kings 4:1b

---

2 Kings 4:1-7 tells a story of a widow whose dead husband, who was a man of God, left behind a debt, which was not cancelled by the creditor. Somehow, this money which was owed had to be paid back or her sons' liberty would be taken from them. They would have become slaves for the rest of their lives, if the prophet Elijah had not intervened. If slavery was a good thing, then this woman would not have minded her sons working for the creditor. Fear gripped the woman and

she was prepared to do whatever the Lord instructed her to do in order to preserve her sons' freedom. This is what God through the Prophet Elijah said to the woman after she had followed his instructions and acquired an abundance of oil:

> *"...Go, sell the oil and pay your debt*
> *and you and your sons live on the rest."*
> 2 Kings 4:7

DEBT POEM

Debt can cause mental illness
Mental illness can cause debt,
you bet
you regret,
you get hooked
you may be shook,
but come on – you know why
door steps lenders, paycheque shops make you
reach the sky,
want want want – so much temptation
Christmas is coming – got to get in with relations,
park our new car here so all can see
no over there, as you might block the flashing
tree,
what's in the post, a catalogue offer
no love, just a final demand from a creditor,

throw it in the bin, sweep it under the carpet
want want want - come on we got to get our
'needs' met,
where are my cards; store, credit, the lot?
I cut them up, this has got to stop,
you did what? – without even asking!
It's for our own good – let's get out of sin,
would you accept an offer of a hyena in the
house?
Of course not, are you mad, I'd prefer a mouse,
well that's what inviting 'debt' into your home is
like dear
let's now think of the kids, our home, our health
and our future year,
thank God we have now come to our senses
eyes open, giving, savings and less expenses,
we no longer think only of ourselves or how to
keep up with the Jones'
we want to bless others within our means, even if
it means shopping at ALDIs,
we no longer think the bigger the toys the better
the person
instead we set our hearts where our treasure is,
and that's in heaven.

By Tope Teniola 07/12/09
© Copy Right 2009

I had a situation as an undergraduate where I was given bad advice, after visiting my former bank manager because of a £250 / about $380 USD overdraft. At the age of 19 years, I agreed for the debt to go to the debt collectors, which meant, technically I was bankrupt. I had to repay the total sum back by way of monthly instalments of £2. This led to a poor credit record which lasted 12 years. This did not teach me a lesson as I incurred further debts years later until I received the revelation from God in 2004 about the state of my heart coupled with my lack of knowledge about how to manage my money and why. After this divine revelation about debt, I became debt free by the grace of God within 6 months, like this widow in 2 Kings, and I have never looked back since. Although the Government cannot force people to better control their spending, more needs to be done to ensure the younger generation are aware of the effects of over spending and shown how to take control of their finances, so they have the opportunity to take responsibility if they want to. I am therefore, currently campaigning for change within our education system in the UK. It has been over 5 years now since the Lord gave me a revelation about debt. As well as publishing a book about debt, I am involved in both the prevention and cure side of debt in my full time job. I not only see the UK debt statistics (UK personal debt over **£1.4 trillion,** more than the African, Asian and

South American continental debts put together) but on a weekly basis, I see the effects of those figures on real lives.

Debt has become an epidemic in our nation and the global economic crisis is not helping. Many of those who were heavily dependent on credit before the 'Credit Crunch' are now leaning to family, friends, high street Pay Cheque/Pawn shops, Door Step Lenders and Loan Sharks. It has become increasingly hard to know who to trust, as more unscrupulous organisations claiming to be debt advisers/consolidators are rearing their ugly heads and preying on the vulnerable in society.

Debt and money worries have been cited as the cause of relationship breakdown in 70% of cases. In the US, 74% of women who had abortions, said it was because they could not afford their babies *(Perspectives on Sexual and Reproductive Health, 2005, 37[3]:110-118)*. Debt and money problems creep into almost every other aspect of our lives including family, employment, housing, health, social and our liberty. It affects the decisions we make in life about the now and the future. What is sad, is many of the young adults from average income households, who wish to better themselves, see no alternative than to take out student loans and leave university with over £25,000 debt each. The cost of living is rising and many struggle on the same salary from year to year or on benefits, which lock them into the 'poverty trap', which is a form of slavery for many. What is even sadder is that some people, who have been drowning in debt, have resulted in committing suicide.

It is fair to say, the UK Government has taken note to a certain extent and has started to fund the third sector to provide free and confidential help for more of those who are over-indebted. But one could argue that it is not enough.

My Vision:

- Not one day in the week goes by without the area of debt/money and linked issues being saturated in prayer

- To see the salvation of multitudes through money ministries

- To see debt/money education (Financial Capability) taught as a compulsory stand alone subject in every school in UK by 2012

- To witness a Year of Jubilee/Personal Debt Cancellation in the UK, spreading to the entire World by 2050 (Love & Forgiveness born through the fear of God, as in Leviticus 25 & Isaiah 61:2)

Between 2007 to 2009 I coordinated prayer for Stewardship's former UK Volunteers Network. Today I continue to lead a strong and faithful team of prayer warriors, chosen by God.

As you can see, the need and the task are colossal and require a coming together as we intercede for our nation as a whole. 5 years on since my revelation about debt, the following scripture keeps resounding in my heart every time I enquire of the Lord about the issue we are facing today in our society:

> *For the love of money is a root of all kinds of evil, for which some have strayed from the faith in their greediness, and pierced themselves through with many sorrows.*
> *1 Timothy 6:10*

I believe the Lord wants His Church as it was in the book of Acts. In many cases there is no real difference between the churches and the world in terms of serving two masters. This amounts to idolatry and goes against the first and greatest commandment. I believe God is raising up champions in our nation who will take the baton and run with it until they light the torch. The Church is meant to be the beacon in this world where the world looks to us and not the other way around. Jesus has all the answers. I believe new churches will be planted based on God's financial principles, teaching the young and the old how to be true stewards. Existing churches will also come into repentance and those who are afflicted through the consequences of debt or the love of money will flock to the Church. There is a coming revival in our land and God wants His Bride to be ready.

The Bible is also very clear on the power of the prayer of agreement. Jesus tells us in Matthew 18:19; *"Again I say to you that if two of you agree on earth concerning anything that they ask, it will be done for them by My Father in heaven"*. He goes on to say, *"For where two or three are gathered together in My name, I am there in the midst of them"*.

I have organised a place where intercessors can come together regularly in one accord to pray for our nation as of January 2010.

> *"If My people who are called by My name will humble themselves, and pray and seek My face, and turn from their wicked ways, then I will hear from heaven, and will forgive their sin and heal their land. Now My eyes will be open and My ears attentive to prayer made in this place."*
> *2 Chronicles 7:14-15*

Here is a trustworthy saying which popped into my spirit in 2007:

"A car is only as good as the supply of petrol."
~ *Tope Teniola*

I also had a petition in circulation for the UK Government to prioritise the provision of Financial Capability as a compulsory stand-alone subject within the Personal Social and Health Education (PSHE) subject for all children under 19 years of age, to fully ensure their future relationships, health, social, economic welfare and liberty do not suffer through a lack of knowledge.

I am pleased to say this campaign and along with pressure from others have helped make a difference for the next generation in our society and beyond. We must speak up for those who cannot speak for themselves (Proverbs 31:8). We must gather together and intercede for our nation in the belief that God Almighty will intervene and deliver His people and heal our land. I am sure the children of Israel cried out to God whilst in captivity in Egypt and God heard and answered through His servant Moses. I believe the African slaves cried out to God Almighty and God took compassion and used Abraham Lincoln to do his part in America, William Wilberforce to do his part in England and others whose names may not be in the History books, but God knows who they are. We must not underestimate the power of prayer. Although we should be praying for ourselves, the Church already has salvation, therefore, we must corporately pray for the World. Not only for the injustice to stop but for the oppressors to hear the word, be cut to the heart and believe, repent and be saved.

Hence, it is never too late for slave owners and murderers and the like to repent. The late John Newton, former slave owner, who wrote the famous song 'Amazing Grace', published 1779, repented and gave his life to Jesus. His heart was transformed over night.

So what was going on in Joseph's head? One can only imagine fear, confusion, and pain from rejection. I believe his brothers were unable to make eye contact with him whilst standing around waiting for any offer of money to get rid of him. Surely Joseph would have realised that his brothers were just as fearful that Joseph's dreams may come true and they would not be able to handle the manifestations of such dreams. They hated him too much. If they were not going to kill his flesh then they certainly wanted to crush his soul and spirit. These were extremely angry and cold hearted young men who were able to eat whilst plotting their younger brother's murder. I do not believe Jacob would be able to recognise his sons, if he had witnessed all of this. The reality of this happening would have broken Jacob's heart.

In life there is always a fine line most people with a good conscience are careful not to cross. Sin is sin; let us not put it in a hierarchy. But how much further we go in our sins, depends on our relationship with God and how much we allow ourselves to be accountable to fellow believers. Many Christians have gifts but lack character. Pride prevents us from having other men and women of God in our lives for Godly counsel. King David is a good example. Although the Prophet Nathan was around, there was a period in David's life where he seldom went to him for counsel. He was able to get away with not doing the will of God and relish in his sin. As one sin led to another sin, David's heart grew harder and harder until he became so entangled in sins that he could not even see the fine line he should not have crossed before receiving help from a man of God.

> *Beware, brethren, lest there be in any of you an evil heart of unbelief in departing from the living God; but exhort one another daily, while it is called "Today," lest any of you be hardened through the deceitfulness of sin.*
> *Heb3:12-14*

Joseph's brothers started off with jealousy, then gossip, which led to deeper envy and malicious gossip. Gossip is like a disease, the gossipers are infected and it spreads rapidly. When this takes place in any family setting, especially in the church, there must be a proper sanctification before the Holy Spirit can move effectively through that church. Gossip breeds hate and envy and leave new believers puzzled – not being able to make a distinction between the Body of Christ and the world. Gossip is self destructive and is something we should leave in the world when we are born again Christians.

> *And do not be conformed to this world, but transformed by the renewing of your mind......*
> *Romans 12:2*

When Joseph's brothers sold him, they also sold a piece of their soul to the devil. They opened the door for serious enemy attack and arguments placed in heaven over their names. This is how each blessing Israel later gave to his sons in Genesis 50 was able to transpire. Not that anyone told Israel what was in the hearts of his sons during this time but God knew.

We are all 'Free in Christ.' God has given us all a free will from the beginning of time. The enemy hates our freedom because he has not got freedom like ours. None of the angels were made in the image of God according to His likeness. Only humans can claim this truth.

> *Stand fast therefore in the liberty by which Christ has made us free, and do not be entangled again with a yoke of bondage.*
> *Galatians 5:1*

Religion and faith are two separate things. Both are seen in a person's lifestyle, however, in a religious lifestyle there is found legalism and bondage, whilst a person who walks by faith is free in Christ. He or she is under grace and not law. This is a very deep subject, which I am not going to go into much detail. However please read Paul's letters in Romans and Galatians. My life experiences, coupled with the Word of God have opened my eyes to this truth. Some people in churches are bound by religion and completely oblivious to it. I used to be one of these people but I thank God He has set me free. It was a matter of 'church goer .V. Relationship with Daddy God.' When I was 16 years of age, I wanted to return to the relationship I had with God during my tender years. With the encouragement of my father, I returned to our local church. As mentioned in an earlier chapter, my confirmation classes did not answer all my searching questions, so during my confirmation service,

I made a declaration with my head but not with my heart. This is dangerous because it gives an outward appearance of holiness but inside, there is no real conviction and still thoughts of having one foot in the church and one foot in the world loomed overhead. My heart was hard and unhealed. I was still in bondage and a carnal Christian. I eventually made Jesus the Lord of my life in 2001 and needed so much healing from my past. The Holy Spirit worked deep within me, bringing revelation by revelation. I must say it has been a journey. I had to be conscious not to revert back to religion in the church. Sometimes the only way we think we will be accepted by others is to behave in a certain way and to criticise those who behave differently in the church. The Lord soon rid me of all of that and changed me from within, not the other people. I was then able to take my eyes off of man and fix them on Jesus. My relationship with Jesus grew more intimate and I truly worshipped Him in spirit and in truth. Be on your guard against distraction in the church. Do not allow anyone to take your eyes off of Jesus, the author and perfector of our faith.

> *"Therefore if the Son makes you free, you will be free indeed....."*
> *John 8:36*

> *For you did not receive the spirit of bondage again to fear, but you received the Spirit of adoption by whom we cry out, "Abba Father."*
> *Romans 8:15*

Freedom and not restraint needs to be encouraged in all the churches. I have attended a church where there was no freedom whatsoever. Even to think for yourself was frowned upon. One had to go to their leader for direction in every aspect of their life. God was not in the equation.

> *Cursed is the man who trusts in man and makes flesh his strength......*
> *Jeremiah 17:5*

> *Blessed is the man who trusts in the LORD, and whose hope is the LORD.*
> *Jeremiah 17:7*

When I discerned something fundamental was missing from this particular former church, I got a strong conviction to leave. I found a Holy Spirit filled church and much healing and deliverance took place in me. I was set free from spiritual bondage.

> *Now the Lord is the Spirit; and where*
> *the Spirit of the Lord is, there is Liberty.*
> *2 Corinthians 3:17*

However, freedom does not mean disorder. God is a God of order and not confusion. Hence why the Apostle Paul advised us on how we should conduct church services.

Chains physically removed do not mean a person is free if inside they do not have a true relationship with God. Similarly, a person in chains, who knows God will know freedom deep within. Suffering can either drive you further away or closer to God. I believe Joseph's experience brought him closer to God and he allowed God to work within him.

> *The Lord was with Joseph, and he*
> *was a successful man; and he was in*
> *the house of his master the Egyptian.*
> *Genesis 39:2*

When the enemy sees a child of God free and successful, he wants to mess that person up. The bible says:

> ....*"Now salvation, and strength,*
> *and the kingdom of our God, and*
> *the power of His Christ has come,*
> *for the accuser of our brethren, who*
> *accused them before our God day*
> *and night, has been cast down."*
> *Revelation 12:10b*

False Accusations, come when the devil has no witnesses. And even then if he could he will bring false witnesses as he did when Jesus was falsely accused.

> *Then she spoke to him with words like*
> *these, saying, "The Hebrew servant*
> *whom you brought to us came in to me*
> *to mock me; so it happened, as I lifted*
> *my voice and cried out, that he left his*
> *garment with me and fled outside."*
> *Genesis 39:17-18*

Potipher's wife was greedy, promiscuous and manipulating. The spirit of Jezebel was in her. Gentle Joseph in his outward bondage could not get away from her. Although one could argue, Joseph could have fled a lot sooner when no one was in the house.

In the church, the bible makes it clear what we should do if a brother or sister sins against us in Matt 18:15-17.

If your brother or sister says s/he is sorry to have hurt you, accept this. The bible does not say analyse every word and dot the i's and cross the t's. This is not love this is bitterness. When you cannot accept a sorry and you go and murmur, gossip and slander that person to whoever will listen in the church, you open the door to the enemy, which leads to contamination in the flock. Only the spiritual will discern what is going on and should pray. If someone is in leadership and has a relationship with the bitter person, he or she should disciple that embittered sister or brother, until deliverance comes.

When there are false accusations flying around in church towards a brother or sister and that person feels bound to be there due to duties in the church, The Lord will vindicate and bless that person. If the accusations are too much for that person to bear, the Lord Himself will deliver that person out of that church into another church where they can not only continue their ministry in peace but also where they can thrive. At times where there is a majority of immature Christians or carnal Christians gathering together, there will be much gossip and back biting. This is very unhealthy and a seriously big obstacle for kingdom advancement. So the Lord will use that godly person elsewhere, while He works on the immature church. Joseph may not have realised at the time that going to prison was the start of another ministry for him as part of his preparation for the fulfilment of what was written.

> *"No weapon formed against you shall prosper, and every tongue which rises against you in judgement you will condemn. This is the heritage of the servants of the Lord, and their righteousness is from Me,"* says the LORD
> Isaiah 54:17

Sometimes, accusations within the family, church, workplace or neighbourhood can sow guilt and discouragement into the person at the receiving end. Even if you made a genuine mistake, you could spend all your time thinking up words to say how sorry you are to a particular person. Joseph may have been in this position when he was being sold for slavery. The person may still not be satisfied with your apology, so further guilt sets in. This happened to me once, where I realised I was thinking as a perfectionist would, as though mistakes should never be made in ministry. So I became so guilty and even worse if the person clearly did not accept my sorry. The Lord told me this type of guilt is idolatry. When I was shown this I quickly repented and moved on in my heart. I have come to terms with the fact that it is impossible to please everyone and I certainly cannot heal someone overnight in my own strength and cause them to forgive. Only God can do this. I now know why Pastor Benny Hinn said he had to form a thick skin in ministry. My greatest role model in this area so far is Sister Maria Etter, who was one of the most criticised female ministers in her time (17th Century). She never retaliated or focused on the critics or the people behind the criticism; she just kept on working diligently for God, led by the Holy Spirit.

After false accusations have been spread about you, promotion may not be immediate but it will come as God is a God of justice.

Joseph was a slave and worked as though working unto the Lord.

> *If you endure chastening, God deals*
> *with you as with sons; for what son is*
> *there whom a father does not chasten.*
> *Hebrews 12:7*

* * *

Chapter 9

Using Your Gifts in Prison

Then Joseph's master took him and
put him into the prison, a place where
the king's prisoners were confined.
And he was there in the prison.
Genesis 39:20

I believe in the Prison is where God does the most character forming in His children. Satan is the accuser, he accuses the Church day and night.

Jesus Christ is the opposite; He is the Great High Priest, our advocate in heaven. For every accusation, Jesus lifts up the saints and pleads on our behalf, constantly reminding The Father of all the faithful things we have done and will do, in His name.

As Portipher's wife was used to accuse Joseph and spread lies about him in order to ruin his good name, Jesus, The Great High Priest was interceding for him.

God allowed Joseph to be put in the confines of prison walls ultimately for His glory. One might ask why Joseph had to suffer so greatly. It seemed as though he was jumping from the frying pan into the fire. Well yes, that is just it. The only place we can be refined for God to bring us into our destiny is through the fire. Gold is refined in this way and we are God's treasures.

Being imprisoned is another form of slavery, except one is in the confines of secure walls. At first, this must have felt daunting for Joseph, perhaps a feeling of Déjà vu. Similar to slavery, when we are imprisoned, we cannot make plans for the future. In fact to plan ahead seems meaningless and even frustrating, as one does not even know if they will live to see the day of their release. Job's plans were wiped out in a day when he lost all (see Job 1). The only words he may have been saying in his heart according to his faith is 'it is well with my soul.' That is why in the book of James, we are taught to say, 'if it is God's will, I will do this and do that.' Living in the Western world or in a circle of wealth, such words do not come natural. Sometimes we can become arrogant in our riches to the extent where we are not even aware we tend to wear pride as a garment instead of humility. It is all about Jesus and it is the Lord's plans which always prevail, so He gets all the glory.

The Lord cannot work with constantly proud people because they will never see things His way. Most proud people work in their own strength. Not that the Lord does not love them; as the Lord always loves the sinner but not the sin. I have had my own experience of pride. I remember I used to look down on single mothers when I was married. I had conservative views, which made me show no compassion for those who had misfortunes in life. Although I experienced dysfunction in my family, I was of the impression that if I could graduate from university, get married before having a child and work in a lucrative field, then so could everybody else. I am so glad my bubble was burst and I was knocked off of my high horse. I do not even like the person I used to be deep inside. Most of my former mindset came from insecurity. So God had to do a great healing in me at the same time of refining. It took years. But God saw I was worth it. During those years, my prison experience came in the form of the 4 ugly D's: Divorce, Debt, Depression and Despair. These are similar iniquities the men who followed David into the cave to be with him, were facing in <u>1 Samuel 22:1-2</u>. David was in his cave after fleeing the wrath and false accusations of King Saul, someone he had once loved and trusted. When the enemy strikes and you have your guard down, this is what can happen. Even in David's prison, God used him to bring hope to desperately needy men from the city. They knew there was nothing for them under King Saul's rule in the city. They knew they needed God but did not quite know how to find Him in the madness of war. Just like Ruth wanted to follow Naomi because where Naomi's God is, is Life; the men who followed David had a similar mindset. In later chapters, we read how some of these men went on to become mighty men of valour.

The story of my divorce is a book in itself. All I can say is at that point the solicitors involved in my case concerning both divorce and child custody told me our case was one of the worst they had taken on. The complexity of the case would have sent any normal woman mad or to an early grave. For me the increased debt, depression and despair followed as I tried desperately to keep sane because of my son, who was only 6 years old at the time. I was not born again when I separated from my former husband. I gave my life to Jesus two years later, after a point of reaching my lowest ebb. I felt like a lonely misfit and wanted to end my life. I was desperate for love and used to look for this in men. This left a deeper spiritual hole in my heart as I went from one man's arms into another. It was at this lowest point in my life, when I realised I cannot refrain from sleeping with another man without the help of God. One friend gently showed me the way back into Jesus' loving arms again and after having a series of bible studies, I was cut to the heart and baptised. I knew in my heart although I can never be perfect, I will never turn away from my First Love again. Most separations do not happen overnight. Resentment is built up over a period of time on both sides. It may be the husband and wife were incompatible; grew apart; or did not seek Godly counsel for their marriage. Whatever the reason, it is important to acknowledge, the enemy is against marriages. I would honestly say 'the love of money' also had much to do with my marriage break up. The foundation of family is based on marriage. The Lord has always intended One Family from the beginning. Family is at the core of His heart. He created us to be in family. But just like our earthly mother and father cannot force us to remain in relationship within our respective families, nor will our Father in heaven force His children to stay within The Family (The Body of Christ). We all have a free will. Divorce is like tearing a sheet of paper in half, leaving jagged edges. Both parties are left to walk around like wounded soldiers. Anger and bitterness is usually formed in even the most amicable separations.

During my divorce process, I went through 5 years of *annus horriblis*. The attacks from the enemy intensified from year to year. The separation and divorce did not warrant the type of persecution I was under. Let me say, I passed through the valley of Bacca (psalm 84) and required serious healing and deliverance afterwards. I would not want my worst enemy to go through what I went through. But God knows His reasons for allowing such a mess in my life. When I attended a support group for those whose relationships had irretrievably broken down, I found after some weeks that I was the only one not on the drug Prozac. The Lord showed me some years after this was because I replaced Prozac with the Word of God. I chose to drink from the fountain of life instead of getting addicted to a man made drug. The bible, no one can master because it is new everyday. The Word of God is more superior than any doctor or surgeon; as no doctor or surgeon can fix our soul and spirit. Only the One who made us can do this. If it were not for my God, I would not be here to tell this tale in the first place. I now have deep compassion for those going through divorce and those who are single parents. I have preached a message and ministered to bring healing to divorcees and single parents. A copy of this tape can be ordered by sending an email.

> *But the Lord was with Joseph and showed him mercy, and he gave him favour in the sight of the keeper of the prison. And the keeper of the prison committed to Joseph's hand all the prisoners who were in prison; whatever they did there, it was his doing. The keeper of the prison did not look into anything that was under Joseph's authority because the Lord was with him; and whatever he did, the Lord made it prosper.*
>
> *Genesis 39:21-23*

It is said Joseph spent at least 2 years in prison. God will allow you to be in your prison for as long as it takes for Him to refine you. Even if it means only 1 year of your life is left before you meet with Him and is spent in your ministry, glorifying Him. Or if it means a powerful part of your ministry is to be carried out in prison like the Apostle Paul, who used his gift of writing in the prison. As a result, the churches of those days and generations after have been and are currently being edified. The churches of the future will also be edified due to Paul's using his gift in prison, until Christ returns.

I would say the 4 ugly D's appeared in the first half of the period I was in my prison, which lasted about 4 years. This I would call the healing part of God's work in me, and then the next phase of my prison is where the Lord released my spiritual gifts. I was not ready to be released from prison yet because I still walked in religiosity and pride. Things looked brighter as I birthed my cell group in 2004. Although I was not released from my prison, the Lord divinely led about 18 women within months, who were also in their own prisons, to the cell group I led and He used me to release them into their destinies; some went on to birth their own cell groups. There was a supernatural multiplication taking place within and throughout my ministry and I was lost for words. I knew it could only be God. Within a short space of time, I was invited to join the church leadership and was given other positions of authority within the church. The Lord was clearly with me, constantly reminding me of His unconditional love and favour.

In the latter parts of your time in prison, God is
1. Humbling you; and
2. Training you.

During this time, like any other human being, I suspect Joseph was wondering to himself:
1. 'Will my gift ever be noticed or even remembered?'
2. 'When will the prophecy over my life come to pass?'

> *And they said to him, "We each*
> *have had a dream, and there is no*
> *interpreter of it." So Joseph said to*
> *them, "Do not interpretations belong*
> *to God? Tell them to me, please."*
> *Genesis 40:8*

Joseph even said 'please'. This is how we should be fanning into flames our gifts even in prison, by asking someone who is desperate for a revelation of God in their lives, if we can use our gifts to help them move forward. Joseph was able to use his gifts within the confines of his prison. Remembering visions and dreams which bring comfort is beautiful. But when a vision/dream also increases ones faith; that is powerful. When I remember the two main visions of my life so far, my faith for witnessing is increased. I am an Evangelist at heart and because I have heard with my ears and seen with my eyes, I cannot help but want to tell the world Jesus is alive! He has prepared a special place for us where there will be no more suffering, weeping, or death. Revelations 21.

So Joseph knew the interpretations of the dreams were from God but was unsure when they would come to pass. He knew his freedom was linked to his gift coming to light and his stepping out of prison and walking in faith according to the promise of God.

If you have not seen or heard audibly, do not be concerned because we all have the Word of God.

> *Blessed are those who have*
> *not seen but yet believe.*
> *John 20:29*

Sometimes we feel forgotten by God and abandoned by man in our prisons. I will never forget, still in my prison, still obediently feeding God's young babies with 'breast milk' (i.e. this a term) used by a visiting prophet describing my cell, when he referred to what the Lord had called me to do while I wait for further direction from Him), and on the final stages of writing my first book, I hit a crossroads in my faith.

One Thursday morning, on 7th July 2005, I was on my usual journey to work. I went up the escalators in Kings Cross underground station and proceeded as usual towards the Piccadilly Line to catch the tube to go to my former job as a freelance Management Accountant in Covent Garden. By then I was already known as the hard working single mother in ministry. As I reached the platform entrance where I would normally go through, a tall station guard stretched out his hand and stopped me from going past and started to close the gates. By then I was already about to run late as it was about 8.55am and I was due to start work at 9am. This as you can imagine really annoyed me as I looked at him displeased 'he' was going to add insult to injury concerning my issue at that time of unpunctuality. He could see I was not pleased so he said, "you have to go around to the other entrance to avoid overcrowding." I tutted in irritation because I usually get in the first carriage and did not like the thought of having to walk all the way around just to get on the same train. I heard the train pull up as I started walking around to the middle entrance, so I ran and pushed my way through to get onto the end of the third carriage. I will never forget that journey for as long as I live because God showed Himself true in the midst of the hassle and tussle of my life. I squeezed into the carriage and we stood there like sardines for at least a minute. Before the doors closed, one woman also desperate to get to work squeezed her way in but it looked hilarious because there really was nowhere for her to stand and still maintain her dignity. I looked at another passenger and we both smirked at the sight.

I remember thinking to myself, I have never seen it so packed in the four and half years I was in this job. The time was about 3 minutes past 9 now and I was getting agitated. "Come on, come on." I thought. Then at last the doors managed to close. We proceeded slowly through the tunnel. Then about 1 minute into the journey between Kings Cross station and Russell Square, I heard the loudest blast I have ever heard in my life. My heart skipped a beat as I instantly thought the train had crashed and remember saying to myself, "this is the last time I'm ever going to take London Transport." I said this because I thought at the time the train had collided with another train due to incompetence. Then I thought I imagined it but was wrong when I saw a thick dark puff of smoke gushing through the carriage from the front like a gale force wind. At the same time, there were loud bangs and sounds of glass shattering, one after the other, as I heard yells and screaming. It did not seem real; as I had never experienced anything like it, it was like a nightmare. I remember closing my eyes and clearly saying what I thought was my last prayer: "Lord I commit my spirit into your hands."

I actually thought that was the end of my life on earth. Then the train came to a silent stand still.

I heard screams and shouts from the carriages in front of my carriage. I opened my eyes and found I was still standing and was not dreaming. By now the whole carriage was pitch black as the lights went out and because of the dense smoke. I began coughing along with many others and my eyes started to sting. I did not say much to begin with as I was in shock but a few of us started to make conversation, like "open the window." "Have you got a light/torch?" "It's ok, you will be alright, and someone will rescue us." After about 5 or 10 minutes, we heard the driver's speaker box make a high pitch noise like a siren. This was one of the saddest parts of this horrible experience for me. I knew the driver of the train was trying to get through to the passengers to speak but the machine was damaged. Then it clicked off and there was silence. I kept saying, "how about the driver, how about the driver?" We all waited for help for what seemed like hours, but was probably actually about a 45 minute wait. I thought to myself within this time, "if the blast had not killed us, the smoke will"; as I remembered the words of the Doctor who tended to my family after our near death experience in the fire at home. I recalled what a lovely time I had with the Lord that same morning before going to work. We had a great fellowship during my quiet time with him.

By this time I began to feel as though a new phobia was trying to oppress me; I just wanted to break out of that dark *prison*.

Some time later, we at last heard voices which came from outside the carriage and could see the reflection of torches. They passed messages to those in the back carriages to pass onto to us. The message was along the lines of, 'we are going to let you out and lead you to safety through the tracks. We have to turn off the tracks first.' I remember breathing a sigh of relief and knew I would live to tell the tale. As we were led through the tracks to safety, I saw a few of the wounded passengers from the first two carriages being led out quickly to get urgent attention. One had blood all over his face and could not walk by himself. As we walked in a single line along the dark and dreary tunnel, I kept asking myself; 'what about the driver' as my heart went out for him/ her; I sensed death.

As I proceeded up the steps into daylight, I cried at the sight of a blue sky, fire engines, ambulances and police helicopters all ready to do their job. There was absolute chaos as journalists were buzzing all over. I walked past one of the news cameras still dazed and without realising. I was later told by a friend he saw me on the main news. I managed to get through to a couple of people on my mobile, including the director of the company I worked for. He made an attempt to collect me from outside Kings Cross tube but had to turn back because he was not allowed past a certain area. Those who could walk were told to make our own way to the nearest hospital. I was able to make a few phone calls to people to tell them what had just happened, a man who recognised me on the tube walked with me for part of my journey to the Whittington Hospital. We talked about our experience and showed each other a photo of our children. I used this opportunity to share my faith with him. He was a Muslim but did not practice. I told him about the beautiful fellowship I had with our Father that same morning and how I knew if I was taken, I would have met with my Lord that morning. He was shaken into doing something about his faith, so I invited him and his family to my church. At this time I still thought our train had crashed. It was not until we approached Euston Station, we heard of other tubes in a similar incident as ours did I start to suspect something. Then one policeman who thought we knew about the truth behind what had happened asked if we were on the bus number 30 which blew up. I looked at him in horror and when he realised I had no idea it was a bomb that caused this chaos, I broke down and cried like a baby. The man I walked with consoled me and sat me down. I was in a further state of shock as I thought of my loved ones.

I also tried to get through to my son's school but all the phone lines by then were jammed. I and the man who the Lord brought to my side to comfort me, exchanged telephone numbers then we went our separate ways to try and go to our respective hospitals.

I kept stopping at a phone booth trying to call my son's school and my parents. I eventually got hold of my step mum, who for no fault of her own did not seem to understand the scale of what happened. Her words seemed to belittle the whole thing. When I put the receiver down I realised people in our business, can easily forget about the ones we love. We can get caught up in a web, chasing money and position that when we really need to be there for others, we are blinded to even the greatest need. I am not referring to my step mum because she is far from insensitive. She is one of the most loving Godly Christian step mums anyone can find. I am talking about the fast and distant culture of me, me, me; we have all, including myself been guilty of.

I felt alone as I hung up the receiver, and continued to walk with my head down in despair, feeling neglected. I was well aware my whole body was covered in soot and every time I blew my nose, black soot appeared on the tissue. I believe I walked about 5 miles and in a state I arrived at the Whittington hospital. The nurses and staff were already waiting outside to attend to us, all we had to do was give our name and we were shown in. When I reached the first attendant, all I could say was my name and date of birth, and then I collapsed into her arms. I was on the hospital bed for about 4 hours with an oxygen mask on and being treated for shock. The nurse gave me all the time I needed to get ready to wait for my friend, Valda's husband to collect me and take me to my son's school. As I got dressed in my hospital room and went on my knees to pray. I asked God what it was He wanted me to see. Why was I meant to witness blood from the wounded and stories of death around me in the hospital and not one part of my body had a scratch?

The truth is the Lord knew of my usual routine to work and that if I went on the first carriage as normal, I would have either been among the badly injured or the dead. No one walks from that incident the same person as before. This was a turning point in my life. It was as though something was impregnated in me, which was waiting to give birth at the right time.

I eventually got to my son's school to ask the teacher to help prevent his dad, who refused to talk to me, from taking him on the tube that day in order to try and protect them both. I received one of the hardest rejections of my life. My son's dad, who is divorced from me, having been informed of what had happened to me by the head of year, completely ignored me, walked past and took our son in a taxi and drove off. This cut me like a knife and left a greater wound in my heart than the actual incident itself. The enemy was really stepping up gear to see me destroyed that year. He sought to do this through rejection and abandonment. The enemy wanted me to feel so deflated like an outcast, in the hope I would give up. Instead of being bitter or giving up, I went home by myself full of forgiveness towards my former husband, got in the shower to wash off all the soot, and I gave thanks to God for my life and promising to continue with Him to destroy the works of the enemy.

I was asked to give my testimony in the church 3 days after the incident, which I did. The Pastor had been praying for the protection of the flock about 8 weeks prior to the disaster due to a vision he said he was given by God about terrorists in the UK. That same Sunday, after the church service, I baptised one of my cell members, Anna, in a pool in her back garden. I had recently led her to the Lord and she was insisting not to wait for her water baptism. The Pastors gave me permission to baptise her. Those who were present had an awesome time in the Lord. Today both her and her husband are saved and in leadership. Anna herself is now the children's Pastor in that church.

A counsellor from Victim Support came to visit me during the time when I had a little false guilt about why I was alive and others had died and were already buried. He said he believed this was a turning point in my life as I had the answers to life. He said he had never seen any of the victims he looks after so positive. Then a detective who visited me for questioning said something even more profound; he said he found comfort in talking to me as he himself was overwhelmed by the whole thing. I shared my faith and invited him and his family to church, which he was open to but never actually came.

Some people at that time, who were not even inside of the train like me, told me they were afraid to travel by London Transport. Since the news of the disaster, some people said it reminded them of 9/11 in the US. I soon learnt I was in the worse of the many disasters which happened that 7/7 morning. The Kings Cross train was reported to have the most deaths and fatal injuries because the bomb was the largest one. For the first 2 weeks, I had a doctor's certificate because of fear and anxiety to travel, especially on the London Transport. I used to walk through the back streets to avoid being near the main road to go to my General Practitioners. My doctor offered me drugs, which I refused to take. The Government organised qualified Counsellors, who have dealt with war victims to give me free counselling.

Grateful as I was, this did not work. I testify today, the Lord helped me to supernaturally overcome fear of London Transport soon after 7/7, only by the power of the Holy Spirit during a Benny Hinn Crusade in the North of England. In fact, my son Christian was also healed from the trauma of his parent's divorce and custody battle at that same crusade. In my spirit, I received words from the Holy Spirit who instructed me to travel by tube on my own the next day in order to attend Pastor Benn Hinn's dinner for leaders, which was to be held in the West End of London. I cried so much at receiving these words spoken so gently to me by the Holy Spirit. I obeyed God by doing exactly that. I knew if I had my own way, I would have asked at least three of my friends to come with me so I could hold onto them. The following day when I got in the tube confidently, the enemy tried to play on my mind as I looked at a Middle Eastern looking man with a large bag on the floor. But I felt our Lord Jesus Christ sat beside me. Although I could not see Him I sensed His peace which surpasses all understanding fill my heart. I am totally healed knowing that the devil is a liar and my life and destiny are in the hands of God Almighty and not man or the devil. The enemy was trying to put fear in me, to prevent me from fulfilling my call. 2 Timothy 1:7. I am in and out of the tube and other parts of the London Transport today without even a second thought. I told you one could never leave that tube disaster the same. I am completely healed of the wounds caused by that terrible day for London, because of the healing power of our Lord Jesus Christ. What is impossible for man is not impossible for God.

> *For a righteous man may fall*
> *seven times, and rise again.*
> *Proverbs 24:16*

As a memorial to all those who died in the 7/7 disaster I wrote this poem:

7/7 – A Terrible Day for London

Today is like no other day in my life,
Today was the day I experienced near death
But came away without a scar on my body
Or broken bone on my flesh,
Today was the day I prayed what I thought was my last
prayer on earth,
Today was the day I committed my spirit
Into the hands of the Lord God Almighty,
Today was the day that the Lord,
Yes – God Almighty spared my life,
For His PURPOSE!
Today is the day my life will never be the same,
Today is the day God is sending me out,

Today is the day God is saying to me
'IT IS TIME!'
Today is the day I ask the Holy Spirit
To direct me every inch of the way,
In what He wants me to do to further God's Kingdom
By pointing people to Jesus,
Today is the day I trust God completely
With the welfare of myself and Christian,
While I prepare myself wholeheartedly
For full-time ministry,
Today is the day I surrender my all –
My all-self to JESUS! Amen.

Matthew 24 & Psalm 91
By Tope Teniola 07/07/05
© Copy Right 2005

I also went on to publish my first book. And in obedience, I went into full time ministry towards the end of 2005, launching PJW Ministries. 'PJW' being 'Praise, Joy and Wealth', which is the overall meaning of my name, Temitope Teniola. The full meaning of my name Temitope is, yes wait for it: 'IT IS RIGHT TO GIVE GOD THANKS AND PRAISE FOR BRINGING ME INTO THIS WORLD!' The Lord does indeed have a sense of humour. To some of my family members and a person who I respected in the church, my announcement of going into full time ministry was frowned upon. The encouragement was minimal and discouragement high. Comments were along the lines of: "it does not make sense a woman going into ministry," "I have heard many people say they are going into full time ministry to avoid working." "Why would you throw away all your education?" Little did I or anyone else realise then that the Lord was preparing my current paid job to be included in the package of my full time ministry. God never does things in halves. Even when it does not make sense at the time of Him doing it, we can be confident He knows what He is doing. God was preparing me then with what I know now. So I officially launched PJW Ministries on a low key scale December 2005; inviting only key people in my life who would be supportive of my mission and did not judge me. PJW ministries now incorporates: Money Talks (Committed to delivering Financial Capability to the next generation, so they do not suffer through lack of knowledge); UK Debt and Money Prayer Ministry (covering the issues we face in the UK); The Precious Foundation (helping Orphans world-wide); Evangelism work on the streets; regular giving to serving the poor and homeless. My paid work at my local Citizens Advice Bureau compliments all the above and my salary helps to finance PJW ministry. I trust the Lord will increase my anointing as He increases the tasks ahead. The truth is God's ways are not our ways.

Only He can join the dots on our life map. Our part is to trust and obey.

You see Joseph may have been snubbed and forgotten by man but he was not forgotten by God. People may be jealous of you and hate you. People may mistreat and abuse you. People may speak falsely against you and slander you. Bless and pray for them. People may even forget about you but know this; God has a plan for your life, a plan to prosper you and not to harm you, a plan to give you a hope and a future.

> *Now to Him who is able to do exceedingly abundantly above all that we ask or think, according to the power that works in us, to Him be glory in the church by Christ Jesus to all generations, forever and ever. Amen.*
> *Ephesians 3.20-21*

I have since received a fresh revelation about the meaning of Psalm 91:16. If I had died in the train, I would have gone to be with my Father in heaven and lived throughout eternity with Him. If however it is God's desire I remain on earth, I will live long to declare the works of the Lord. Therefore, I am complete in Him on earth as in heaven.

With long life I will satisfy him
and show him My salvation.
                              Psalm 91:16

Three and a half years on from this disaster, I was a 9-5 working mum; leader at church but still learning, sometimes the hard way, I still require comforting from time to time. I liken life on earth with us being constantly rubbed up and down on a cheese grater. Some periods we are rubbed with more force than the other times. Sometimes we are rubbed in the area of the grater with smaller and sharper holes and at times we land on the smooth part of the grater. Then we are allowed a short break until the next time to be grated like cheese. I have been attacked ferociously by the enemy even from within the church. The enemy will use anyone who gives him an opening and who has access to you. It can make you wonder, 'is it time for me to call it a day' or 'how can those prophecies be true, if I am being treated like this?' Our emotions are placed within our soul. Our soul is so precious and forms part of what makes us complete human beings. Our soul was never meant to be battered and bruised. The Garden of Eden was a place of peace, joy and righteousness, a place where humans and the animals only knew love. However, sin brought the fall and the fall brought misery to mankind. The gift of salvation God has for us is indeed free but on our journey to the Promised Land, the spirit of Amalekites continuously attacks us from behind. Joshua taught God's people to get up and fight for their inheritance. Those who are spiritual must also teach the church to arise and fight for what is rightly ours. Also I believe to keep us from being proud; the Lord allows a thorn in our flesh, just like the one the Apostle Paul asked Him to remove three times. Each thorn will be different for every one chosen to do great things for God. This is so we will only give Him the glory. His grace is indeed sufficient for us. I have watched many people, believers and unbelievers alike, fall apart due to the pressures of life. This is why we must put on God's full armour daily. Ephesians 6:10-18. We are in a battle where it is written, Christ already has the victory. Our part is to endure until the end. Keep giving your testimony of what God has done for you and is still doing in your life. When we have a grateful heart, we notice even the smallest things, where God has intervened or given us the grace to overcome. Your testimony and the blood of Christ is what overcome Satan. Revelations 12:12.

> *"These things I have spoken to you, that in Me you may have peace. In the world you will have tribulation; but be of good cheer, I have overcome the world."*
> *John 16:33*

I believe Joseph felt life was like being on a cheese grater most of his life. He would have most certainly wondered when the Chief Butler would remember his gift. Even when things seemed better after he was released from the prison, promoted and married with children, I truly believe deep down Joseph wondered when and how his dream would come to pass or if ever it would. I believe there were occasions when he laughed at himself or was even disillusioned when he thought of the dream and on top of that, speaking it out to his family, whom he had no idea during his time of what may have appeared as ordinary life' to Joseph that he would ever set eyes on his family again. In fact he did not even know if they were alive. How could they possibly bow down to him? However, who knows whether thoughts of his dreams brought him comfort in times of loneliness or discouragement. It is said we should ponder over the prophecies over our lives. Although it tarry they will come to past and we can be preparing ourselves for them. Isabelle Allum, Prophetess said, when we get prophetic words we should ponder over them and prepare for it to come to pass. She said if a parent who is very close to you instructed you to get ready because they have bought you tickets to go to Africa for something important to them, you would trust them without asking questions and start packing your bags. Well, this is how we should be when we hear words from God, our Father in Heaven. His sheep know His voice. John 10:4. The word Prophet means 'mouthpiece for God'.

When we are getting on with ordinary life and feeling discouraged or rejected, the Lord sometimes helps us remember our dreams and visions which bring comfort to the soul. During 2008, a visiting prophet came to the church where I was fellowshipping and called anybody to the front of the church who wanted to bring a particular sum in the form of an offering to the church building. I first prayed before I got a conviction to go up at the mention of a particular sum. There were about 30 people standing in front of the altar, and I stood behind a couple of people with my head down. All of a sudden there was silence and we all heard the letters 'T O P E' being spelt out. Then some of the congregation gasped and realised the prophet had just spelt my name out slowly, as the prophet visualised each letter. I too gasped and raised my head with my eyes wide open. Then when he asked, "who is that?" The people in front of me moved aside to allow me to pass through to the front. The prophet looked at me and asked my name and I replied "Tope". He smiled and said, I will pray for you tomorrow." He did in fact minister to me along with some more powerful prophetic words the same evening and the day after that. But the greatest comfort from his prophetic words to me was the mentioning of my name. The name that I have been known and called from birth, 'Tope'.

> *"Fear not, for I have redeemed you; I have called you by name; you are Mine."*
>
> *Isaiah 43:1b*

This prophet did not know me and I had never seen him before. He did not know I was going through a rather discouraging time. Nor did he know some of the pain was caused by people within that church. But, God knew. And He was the One who spoke through the prophet to bring comfort, healing and honour before the whole congregation (Isaiah 43:4). I meditated on this scripture when I returned home that same evening; I got on my knees and wept. The presence of God was so strong all around me.

Remember we are in a battle. But God does not sleep. He is the King in the front line going before us. When any of His soldiers are wounded, He looks around and even while the battle is going on, He picks us up, carries us and touches those wounded areas on our body, soul and spirit. He speaks to us lovingly, reassures us of His love and Victory and puts us back on our horse to continue on in the battle until the end. We are overcomers in Him. Thank You Jesus! Thank You Lord!

I was still in transition period from religion to true freedom before the above happened. Not long after that prophecy, I began to dance in front of the church freely, not caring what the congregation thought of me. In fact most times I was in another realm. I simply forgot people were present. The presence of the beauty of God was all around me; joy filled my heart as though I was in heaven. I am always strengthened after worshipping God in spirit and in truth. He is worthy of our praises. Only that year I realised God was about to birth something through me. I was so desperate to truly know what it is like to truly be free in Christ. I could see some people who were comfortable in religion felt uncomfortable with my breaking out of my old coconut shell. Nevertheless, I continued to praise God. Out of me came this poem:

If Only

If only I was in heaven
I'd be like the bird of a raven,
Or like a bird of a magpie
Flying high in the sky,
With my mate near by
Oh why or why
Lord, oh why,
Can't I be as FREE as a magpie in the sky?
Floating on the wind, so strong
Yet so calm,
Where no one in this world can do me harm,
Oh why oh why

If only – I could fly?
Light – FREE,
Flying up in the tree
When I get healed
I wouldn't have to worry – about it being undone,
Cause in heaven – victory is always won,
My destiny is in Your hands Lord
And you told me,
I am who I am
I am whom I'm meant to be,
So, why – oh why
Lord, IF ONLY I could fly,
High, high, oh so high!
Oh Lord – IF ONLY I could fly.

By Tope Teniola 22/04/08
© Copy Right 2008

For some of us still, our prisons are as a result of our stubbornness or disobedience. We are born for a purpose and occasionally on our journey we make a covenant with God. This could be even a rededication of our lives to Jesus. When we do this, God expects something from us. Jonah was a Prophet who had a beautiful intimate relationship with God. Their relationship was unique and one of the only ones where God's sense of humour shines through.

> *Then God said to Jonah, "Is it right for you to be angry about the plant?" And he said, "It is right for me to be angry, even to death!" But the LORD said, You have had pity on the plant for which you have not laboured, nor made it grow, which came up in a night and perished in a night. "And should I not pity Nineveh, that great city in which are more than one hundred and twenty thousand persons, who cannot discern between their right hand and their left – and much livestock?"*
> *Jonah 4:9-11*

I know I used to be a stubborn person and a person who used to procrastinate. Since being in the 7/7 disaster, I pray to God, "Please do not put me in the belly of the whale; I don't want to be in the belly of the whale again. Please Lord show me what you want me to do next; which direction do you want me to take?" I have learnt the hard way that when God is calling you to do something, this may involve you moving onto another territory to do it. If we are comfortable in our current territory (especially for worldly reasons) and disobey God or drag our heels, the Lord will do whatever He has to do to get through to us, in order for us to see how serious He is about a certain mission. The Lord is always with us, no matter how difficult the task. <u>Matthew 28:18-20</u>.

Even Jesus, who is God in the flesh, had a mission on earth and unlike us, never procrastinated. He never lost focus and kept in close fellowship with the Father in this seemingly confused world we live in. Hence, The Father said, **"You are My beloved Son, in whom I am well pleased."** <u>Mark 1:11</u>. God takes His work on earth and in heaven very seriously. He is a God of compassion. He wants us to see His heart, so we can go for Him; turning the hearts of His people back to Him. None of us who are saved and have our own children want to see our children perish. Souls, souls and more souls is God's cry and should also be ours.

※ ※ ※

Chapter 10

❧ You Fit Perfectly ❧

"You shall be over my house, and all
my people shall be ruled according
to your word; only in regard to the
throne will I be greater than you."
                              Genesis 41:40

These are Pharaoh's famous words to Joseph, after he was released from prison. When you have received your training and character building in the prison, divine promotion is around the corner.

Joseph could have been bitter but he chose instead to be better. David is another example of someone who could have been bitter towards King Saul. He sought to ruin his reputation through accusations and slander and even sort David's life due to the spirit of jealousy and anger, just as Joseph's brothers did. But David chose to honour Saul. He did the right thing to flee, as well as made the right decision not to retaliate. God was testing both David and Joseph's hearts, whilst at the same time forming their characters in these extremely difficult situations. This was part of their training. One major bit of advice I will give to all God's elect is to never remain offended; blessed you will be. I had to learn this too. People, even leaders will say or do things which can cause you to become offended. This is very hard to deal with especially within the body of Christ. But take my advice, and like Joseph and David, you will be blessed. Joseph was never forgotten by God in the prison, only God allowed the Chief Butler to forget him because his character had not been properly formed. Joseph would not be able to handle the colossal task of being second in command of Egypt, if there was an ounce of pride or insecurity in him.

God uses the foolish things of this world to confound the wise. How in Pharaoh's right mind would he promote an ex-convict overnight as his right hand man? How can you set a prisoner free because of his gift and put him as Governor of a country? It is unheard of. And to this day has not been repeated. A similar promotion happened with Nelson Mandela in South Africa, when he was set free from prison and several months later he was elected President of South Africa. This was an amazing day in mankind's 20th century history. Nothing similar has yet been repeated. We learnt later Nelson Mandela buried his head in the bible whilst in prison and like Joseph drew near to God. They both chose to forgive their oppressors and wait patiently on God to vindicate them and do justice.

We must never underestimate the power of forgiveness. I would say every single human being needs to be forgiven and learn how to forgive others who hurt them, but most especially God's ministers. If God has called you and you hold something against another individual, first release them in your heart. Your ministry's growth may be stunted if you are holding even the pettiest grudges. If someone continues to hurt you, ask God for wisdom in how to deal with that person but you must forgive them and decide a biblical course of action to put things right.

Of course even after we have forgiven, it does not mean we walk in folly towards those we have forgiven. They may or may not have repented or turned away from their wicked ways. Joseph completely forgave his brothers but he applied wisdom to test the waters in Genesis 42:15. If you normally go for a swim in a lukewarm lake and on the odd occasion, the lake was cold, you would perhaps forget and still dive in every time or first dip your toe in the water to check first. If on one occasion the lake was frozen over with ice, you would most certainly proceed with caution the next time you approach this same lake.

It was now safe for Joseph to step out into what God had for him. Little did Joseph know, the future of Egypt and Israel were in his hands. God was gracious to allow Joseph to see his dream come to pass as his brothers bowed down to him. Genesis 42:6-9. By now Joseph would have learnt to humble himself in the mighty presence of the Lord. He would have adjourned himself with wisdom from the harsh lessons he experienced coupled with his intimacy with our Creator through his suffering. In fact Joseph's suffering could be likened to the suffering of Christ, for the salvation of Israel and the Gentiles. Joseph was born to save a part of the world, a people chosen by God for the Messiah to be born into. Jesus also was born for one core purpose; and this was to save the whole world. Both fulfilled their tasks and fit perfectly in their place in heaven; Jesus Christ, who was and is and is to come, being seated in the highest place. Isaiah 53 and Philippians 2:9-11.

The Lord spoke to me in a dream in 2008 and said, **"I have called you for *purpose* and not *position*."** It did not make so much sense at the time. I was still in leadership in my former church and wondered what this meant. After I had put it to the back of my mind, my heart started crying out for world missions. The Lord was showing me that I was allowing my position as leader to blind me from my core purpose on earth. I then started to feel as though I did not fit in that church's vision and somehow God was preparing my heart to move on in His perfect timing. I had no idea how He was going to orchestrate my transition but for someone who entered into ministry the way I did, I was ready for anything.

What mattered was not what position Joseph reached but that he knew, he fit perfectly.

In March 2008, when I was in Denmark for a friend's wedding, I attended a church there, where the senior pastor of my former church, was invited to minister. During ministry, he instructed me to help minister to one of the women in the front, while his wife, my then leader, was also ministering to the people in the front. I did minister as instructed and the woman thanked me afterwards as something I said set her free within. Then towards the end the pastor continued to minister to the Ministers of that church. So I queued up last to receive ministry. When he prayed for me, he said God was about to show me how to not give in to my insecurities. His wife then came up to me and whispered in my ear, "Ask God to show you what being complete in Him means." I was quite puzzled by the whole thing because I thought my knowing nothing in all creation can ever separate me from God's love through Christ Jesus was sufficient to feel secure all the time. Well for me it obviously was not, due to all I had suffered in the past. The truth is every kind of suffering in the human race can be found in Jesus. Jesus can relate to all suffering because He suffered the most. That is why He has the supremacy. In fact all suffering points us to Jesus.

So, when I arrived back in the UK, I decided to seek God for a revelation of Colossians 2:10.

> *And you are complete in Him, who is*
> *the head of all principality and power.*
> *Colossians 2:10*

As I pressed in through prayer, The Lord gave me a powerful revelation, which I could not contain within me, so although I am no painter, I drew a sketch of what I had seen (Please see below). This is what the Lord showed me: Christ is the Head of the Church and His intention is to save the whole world. Before the foundation of the earth, we were all known to Him. It was never intended that we be separate from Him. He showed me His head then all of a sudden I saw His body in the form of a jigsaw puzzle. There were loads of pieces and some missing pieces. Each one of the over 6 billion people on this planet was represented in this jigsaw and all have a special place in Him. And each one fits perfectly. He then zoomed into my space, and as I looked closely, I could see my name on it and date of birth. I looked at Him and with His eyes He lovingly beckoned me to take my rightful place. So I stepped into my place on the puzzle and as I stood there, there was a release of freedom and power I had never known before. I knew in my spirit that no matter what I have been through in life, I have always belonged to the One whom, through whom, by whom and for whom the World was made. No one can take my place in the puzzle because they just would not fit. Neither could I take the place of another in that same universal puzzle, because I would not fit in their place. I felt the Lord was saying to me, we are all unique in Him. We are all made differently to carry out the purpose for which we were made, to do the work set in advance by Him for us to do. Ephesians 2:10. I felt the missing pieces in the jigsaw body were all those who are lost and God is expecting the found pieces who have taken their place to go out searching for the lost pieces in order to show them their rightful place in the jigsaw puzzle, which is the Body of Christ. I felt the Lord's compassion for His people so strongly. This was not just about me but He was showing me because He wants me to share this with the world.

Different denominations were never God's original intention. We were meant to accept each one as different made for the glory of God. Every genuine Christian has their own unique and beautiful relationship with God. I believe God is crying out for the lost like never before in these end times. Many of us take for granted that we are saved and some even get complacent. All churches must put aside pride, differences and insecurities and partner together to win the lost for Jesus. We also need to stop being inward focused but outward also. You can tell the inward focused churches by their prayer meetings. Test your church. Are your regular prayer meetings only about each other or only about the church service and the pastors? If so there is something fundamentally wrong. We are not kept on earth to glorify the pastors or other members; nor make the pastors famous. We have been left on earth to make JESUS' name famous wherever we go. We are not in church to do politics with the country's government but with the devil and his government. The Good Fight is not about fighting each other or trying to get one over the other, in order to prove them wrong. It is about destroying the works of the devil. The only way this can be achieved is by us fixing our eyes on Jesus, who is the author and finisher of our faith. We must stop being cruise ships but instead lifeboat vessels. We must go out to where the unchurched are and bring the Father's love to them so they can have the opportunity to hear the gospel with open hearts.

I believe the Lord was showing me that the million pieces, which are found secure in Him, must go out and find the billions lost. The Lord was showing me The Great Commission in a way I had never looked at it before. When it is our turn to return in our jigsaw space, that is, to be with the Lord, after our purpose on earth has been fulfilled, He will say, **"Well done, good and faithful servant!...... Come and share your Master's happiness."** Matthew 25:21. He will take us into paradise – which from what I have experienced in a trance back in 2004 is the 'perfect land', a place of absolute joy, security and tranquillity. A place where, when you step into God's bright light, your entire body can not help but ooze with praise for our living God. The world must know our identity is found in our Creator; we ALL fit perfectly. I want to tell the whole world, we fit perfectly! Don't you?

Even Joseph's eleven brothers are complete in Him, but just did not know it at the time. All the twelve brothers' names are written on the gates of heaven. John 4:12 and Revelation 21:12. ...*And the government will be on His shoulders.* Isaiah 9:6b. What the devil meant for evil, God meant for good:

"Now do not be grieved or angry with yourselves because you sold me here; for God sent me before you to preserve life. For these two years the famine has been in the land, and there are still five years in which there will be neither ploughing nor harvesting. And God sent me before you to preserve a posterity for you in the earth, and to save your lives by a great deliverance. So now it was not

> *you who sent me here but God; and*
> *He has made me a father to Pharaoh,*
> *and lord of all his house, and a ruler*
> *throughout all the land of Egypt."*
> *Genesis 45:5-8*

Here Joseph was saying in so many words, 'I fit perfectly in Him'. Joseph was never a misfit, you were never a misfit and I now know I am no misfit. We are all complete in Him; we all fit perfectly, even while God is doing a work within us in order to make us fit for His purpose.

One of the devil's greatest fears is that all the Christians will grasp and live out the full meaning of the following verses:

> *"...that Christ may dwell in your*
> *hearts through faith; that you,*
> *being rooted and grounded in love,*
> *may be able to comprehend with*
> *all the saints what is the width*
> *and length and depth and height*
> *– to know the love of Christ which*
> *passes knowledge; that you may be*
> *filled with all the fullness of God."*
> *Ephesians 3:17-19*

Yet when Jesus returned to sit at the right hand of the Father in heaven, He sent His precious Holy Spirit to be with us and work through us. The Holy Spirit is here as our helper, so we can go in His power and in Jesus' name. He shows us truth; pointing people to Jesus' love in whatever we do. Even when we make mistakes and sin; we point people to the cross of Calvary saying, this is why He died and rose again. This is why we all need Jesus' love.

God fits perfectly, for He is who He is. Satan wanted His place but did not realise he will never fit. Our ultimate covering comes from Christ who has consumed the world.

> *But I saw no temple in it, for the Lord God*
> *Almighty and the Lamb are its temple.*
> *Revelation 21:22*

Back in 2004, I clearly heard, **"Get out of debt and do not look back"** (God's voice received in my spirit) was God preparing me through the power of the Holy Spirit, to be where I am today and for what is to come in the future. The prison of the 7/7 disaster was the incident that catapulted me into birthing my ministry and going full steam ahead to publish my first book, ***Debt Revelation – Do Not Look Back,*** based on hearing the voice of God. Since writing my first book, I have personally led numerous people to the Lord and into a closer relationship with God (including my son Christian – Good Friday, 2007 after showing him the DVD: Heaven's Gates, Hell's Flames); I have Pastored a cell group and a group of 12 leaders, where we witnessed great manifestations of the Holy Spirit; preached and ministered in various churches; led regular evangelistic events for the unchurched (called 'Lunch with Friends'); delivered financial skills for life training to approximately 2,000 individuals and have done what I said I would do in my first book, which was to contact the UK Government on protecting the next generation. I started writing to the Government in 2005 and received replies, which were initially unsatisfactory.

In 2009 I learnt through PFEG (Personal Finance Education Group) of Sir Alasdair Macdonald's recommendations from his review, to make PSHE (Personal, Social, Health and Economic Education) statutory in schools. However, Financial Capability as a component subject within PSHE was not compulsory because teachers could choose which subjects they saw as a priority. I then spoke to the large organisations to see whether they would campaign but one said they had already looked into it and saw it was too complex; I then told them I would start a personal campaign, which I did. I am pleased to say, the latest reply from my correspondence dated 5th January 2010 from Diana Johnson MP (Department for Children, Schools and Families) was the one, which has really blessed my heart to the point of overwhelming tears of joy. Thanks to other like-minded individuals, Financial Capability will now be taught in every UK school within PSHE as a compulsory subject as of September 2011. Jesus always has the Victory and gets the glory. God is a God of justice. Thank you for all those who prayed for me. If you can change one life for the good, you are potentially positively affecting a whole family, community or even nations. When I end each financial capability training session or talk delivered to teenagers, I say to the sixth form and college students, "Your value is not found in your valuables but in who you are, and that's you." Who knows how many Josephs there are in the audience? If Pharaoh had not released Joseph from prison *Israel* would have died. The Lord has a way of preserving His people and you could be responsible for playing an instrumental part. I am now at peace in this whole area, knowing that as I continue to work in schools for the rest of the 2010 academic year; and even if the Lord moves me into the next phase of my call thereafter; it is done! Our children are worth fighting for! As I review my four point vision mentioned in earlier chapter, I can now see God has done two of them; which has strengthened my faith. I know He will do the other two and I will give my testimony for His glory.

The Lord has also used me to train up and supervise more than 50 new staff members, within 6 months which has never been done before in this organisation, in order to meet the growing demand of people seeking general advice and information in the current economic climate we find ourselves in. As a result in the first quarter of 2010, the organisation has seen a 95% increase in new clients being listened to and having their problems dealt with. When you have had a past like mine, you will understand how rewarding these statistics are to me. I hate suffering and I love to defend the rights of the poor and needy. Today I also lead a small team set to deliver financial capability training to hundreds of front line workers. They go on to help thousands in the community and further train multiplied more young adults to prevent them from being trapped in the snare of the enemy. When the Lord is in it and when you remain humble, He Himself will exalt you – of course like Joseph I had to learn humility and I still ask God for the humility of Christ. The Lord has caused people in influential places to headhunt me for photos, press articles, and other PR in this area. People stop to ask, how I do it. I point to heaven. I say 'it is by God's grace' or 'it is God'. They look at me blankly. The truth is I have not had to lift a finger in this area for doors to open. I simply say 'yes Lord' and in my weakness, I walk in His anointing. It is not by might, nor power but by God's Holy Spirit.

I confess, it was really hard for me to step down from the leadership of my former church. Handing over my cell group, which was like my baby, to another person, was one of the hardest things I have done concerning ministry, but I knew God was in it. The truth is, I was no longer feeling fulfilled spiritually in that church. In fact I was in stagnation, and when this happens, it is easy to get bored and distracted. When certain things happened to me, I realised I had to seek God's direction alone before making the hard decision of moving on into the unknown. Moses would have been in a similar place internally. He would have been looking outside the 4 corners of the walls of comfort into the unknown. Yearning on the inside to help vulnerable people. Fed up of the political infighting within Pharaoh's household. Leaving his reputable position behind in order to live for purpose. The truth is, I am only a steward of the cell I birthed and my current ministry. God is the owner. All belong to God and we must surrender all to Him, especially in times when He is moving us on to the next phase of our journey in Him. So, after praying about it, I took the brave move of stepping out in faith and although I love the church members dearly, I have never looked back since. One unknown author wrote: 'Growth means change, and change involves risk, stepping from the known to the unknown'. Abraham did this by faith, and thank God we can use Him as our example of faith today.

> *Brethren, I do not count myself to have apprehended; but one thing I do, forgetting those things which are behind and reaching forward to those things which are ahead, I press toward the goal for the prize of the upward call of God in Christ Jesus.*
> *Philippians 3:13-14*

You see I love the Lord and nothing in all creation can ever change that! The Lord has graciously given me the desires of my heart to step out of my comfort zone, into first, the mission field of the UK soil, where on a weekly basis I now enjoy serving the poor and homeless people in Watford. Yes, there is great enjoyment found through the fulfilment of serving. I do this through a Missions Shaped Community (MSC) church called St Andrews in Chorleywood. The idea of the lifeboat church came from God, planted into the hearts of Mark Stibbe and Andrew Williams. Elaine Dean, one of the founders of this MSC sensed a commissioning over my life to minister to the homeless, so she prayed for me when I was only there to visit, without even knowing the Lord had already spoken to me about serving the poor. Andrew Williams on his day of leaving St Andrews to answer his call to pastor a church in the US said to me "You are special, get rooted in this church". Thereafter at this MSC's outreach, I was asked to minister to a group of more than 40 homeless men and women, sharing a short message, which brought hope, healing and deliverance. Isaiah 61. I also serve on St Andrew's Money Ministry and the church's main Ministry Team. I have no idea how long the Lord wants St Andrew's to be my spiritual home but I will not lean on my own understanding and trust Him, who is all knowing. The irony is one of the first songs I sang at St Andrew's Church on my first visit in April 2009, and which has stayed on my heart like glue is:

JESUS, ALL FOR JESUS,

All I am and have and ever hope to be.
All of my ambitions, hopes and plans,
I surrender these into Your hands
For it's only in Your will that I am free
For it's only in Your will that I am free

1991 Words Spirit of Praise Music

I have now obeyed the Lord's call since 2004, for me to attend bible school, where I am doing a 2 year diploma at New Life Bible School and a distant learning course with Reinhard Bonnke's School of Fire. It is great to be a student of the Word. I love learning and being stimulated in the Word of God, which is living and active, sharper than a double edged sword. Hebrews 4:12; 2 Timothy 3:16-17; and John 1:1.

I was asked to be the Prayer Director for Crown Financial Ministries UK, a UK plant from the largest global ministry teaching God's Financial Principles to millions in over 80 nations. I humbly accepted this role and I can only stand in awe of God for what He is doing in me and through me.

I am back on the streets evangelising regularly; seeking and saving the lost; being the hands and feet of Jesus. My friend and I led a homeless man to the Lord recently. We directed him to a local church and to an Alpha Course. People have asked to join in our street evangelism. I know the Lord is going to expand this ministry of reconciliation. Please lift this in your prayers? I am in talks with pastors of different churches. I no longer only win for a particular church. There is only One Church. The bible simply warns us to be discerning and to keep away from the false prophets, who include, self appointed people in churches twisting scriptures to suit their own hidden agendas; using Jesus' name in vain. This is why the bible says we must test the spirits to see whether they are from God. (1 John 4:1).

The doors have also now opened for worldwide missions. Twice in the past, when I intended to travel to Nigeria for a holiday, my plans were frustrated beyond my control. I did not quite understand this then but now I know God's intention for me was Missions and not a holiday. I have now travelled to Nigeria for my first time November 2009, to visit an orphanage, which has caused me to birth 'The Precious Foundation' a project to help orphans around the world. The Zonal Pastor of the Redeemed Church of God in Abuja told me since my visit to the orphanage, his heart is now to birth an orphanage based on biblical principles in Abuja, through their church. Glory be to God alone. I have since published the first issue newsletter on this mission's trip and others have already come forward to offer donations and help, even on the day of releasing it. The Lord is clearly doing tangible things through my ministry, which I could never do in my own strength. And I know, according to prophecies, I have only scratched the surface; there is much more to come.

My most recent commissioning is where I was asked to coordinate a Psalms Enchanted Evening for the 4th July 2010, the first of its kind recorded in history. Here, some of the Jewish community of the largest Synagogue in Western Europe and Christian Churches came together to listen to a band, choirs from all nations and the well known soloist Ian White, worship God through songs taken from the Psalms. I was also asked to open this great event before local MPs, Councillors and other dignitaries with a poem I wrote, inspired by the Holy Spirit in 2002 titled 'My Psalm 23'. There were 200 people in attendance and all left joyful, inspired and wanting more. Only the Lord could have put such a unique and special event together like this, where Rabbi and Pastors come under one roof; Jew and Gentile, to celebrate our One true living God, before the eyes of the nations. Among the positive comments and feedback, someone came up to me and said, "You have been given honour." I replied, "double honour in place of my shame as it is written in Isaiah 61:7". She smiled. The President of this Synagogue commended my poem and told me he is going to translate it into Hebrew and send to me. I asked if he would also read it out to the congregation in his Synagogue, he said he may just do that. The words of the Lord's Prophets will always come to pass in its season. 'For as the soil makes the young plant come up and a garden causes seeds to grow, so the Sovereign Lord will make righteousness and praise spring up before all nations.' Isaiah 61:11 (NIV).

I write this to encourage you. If your life has been a mess, then you are a walking testimony. God wants to turn your mess into your message. The Lord has set before you an open door, which no man can shut. (Revelation 3:8). I do not boast in myself or my current success and successes to come, but I boast in the Lord, Maker of Heaven and Earth. (2 Corinthians 10:17).

The story of Joseph's life, although seemingly rough to begin with; although he was on that cheese grater, God never left Him. On the contrary, He was working on his character in order to bring him into his true inheritance. (Genesis 49:22-26). Joseph was transformed from a selfish boy to a selfless man. He not only forgave his betrayers but went on to be generous to them by giving them the land of Goshen. He blessed his persecutors and taught foreigners how to live simple lives and out of what they have; how to sow and give, so that others too may reap a harvest in due season. Genesis 45:10 and (Genesis 47:23-25). God is working on your character today. He allows the *pit* experience to shock you; He allows the *prison* experience to mould you; then He will show you how to truly receive and experience His love properly and go forth to bless others with the overflow. You, like Joseph may be the skunk of your brothers and sisters' eyes. The devil may have used people, especially those you love and become vulnerable towards, to reject you and despise you and make you feel unclean and unworthy. They may, having used you, treat you with contempt or as a complete stranger. Love and forgive them; and rejoice, because all the time, our LORD, due to His unconditional LOVE is saying:

"You are complete in Me!"
YOU FIT PERFECTLY!

Tope and Abiole (Youth Leader for Redeemed Church of God, Kubwa) in Abuja Nigeria. November 2009.

And we know that all things work
together for the good to those who
love God, to those who are the
called according to His Purpose.
Romans 8:28

Tope with the some of the orphans aged 0-5, in Abuja
Children's Orphanage. November 2009.

Blessed is the man who endures
temptation; for when he is
approved, he will receive the
crown of life which the Lord has
promised to those who love Him.
James 1:12

My Precious Covering

When I go to bed at night
I need my covers to hold me tight,
They are not just for warmth but comfort too
They help me feel so secure it's hard to go to the loo,
As my shoes protect me from the stones when I walk
My parents watch out for me, at least they ought,
In the real world this does not always happen
Sometimes they are taken away all of a sudden,
By crime; shame; health and death
Disaster, evil, greed and selfishness,
This was not God's intention this I know
The enemy interfered; such evil he did sow,
The world is fallen, dark and confused
Families torn apart, many loved ones we loose,
Yet this does not stop my inner longing
For someone to love me hold me and be my covering,
Desperately I look around
But sadly seems no one to be found,
I cry deep within, my soul in anguish
As I suffer in silence, feeling as though
I'm being punished,
I look upwards to the One who made the stars
He's my only hope as He sees beyond Mars,
He is my hiding place; my refuge and fortress
The One who promised to take me Home away
from this mess

He is the Alpha and Omega, the First and the Last
The One who never left Joseph when
he became an outcast,
Somehow I know when I hear the angels singing
That I fit perfectly under His precious covering.

By Tope Teniola 01/01/2010
© Copy Right 2010

* * *

❧ Appendix ❧

THE GREATEST MIRACLE

Some say the greatest miracle is when someone gives their life to Jesus. Although I agree this is one of the greatest miracles, in my opinion, the greatest miracle of all is **The Resurrection**. Miracles draw crowds, big miracles draw big crowds but great miracles draw great crowds to not just marvel but draw multitudes into worship.

> So when Jesus came, he found that he had already been in the tomb four days. Now Bethany was near Jerusalem, about two miles away. And many of the Jews had joined the women around Martha and Mary, to comfort them concerning their brother. Then Martha, as soon as she heard that Jesus was coming, went and met Him, but Mary was sitting in the house. Now Martha said to Jesus,

"Lord, if You had been here, my brother would not have died. But even now I know that whatever You ask God, God will give You." Jesus said to her, **"I am the resurrection and the life, He who believes in Me, though he may die, he shall live. And whoever lives and believes in Me shall never die. Do you believe this?"** *She said to Him, "Yes, Lord, I believe that You are the Christ, the Son of God, who is to come into the world."*

John 11:17-27

Then they took away the stone from the place where the dead man was lying. And Jesus lifted up His eyes and said, **"Father, I thank You that You have heard Me. And I know that You always hear Me, but because of the people who are standing by I said this, that they may believe that You sent Me."** *Now when He had said these things, He cried with a loud voice, "Lazarus, come forth!" And he who had died came out bound hand and foot with grave clothes, and his face was wrapped with a cloth. Jesus said to them,* **"Loose him, and let him go."** *Then many of the Jews who had come to Mary, and had seen*

> *the things Jesus did, believed in Him.*
> *John 11: 41-45*

> *...and not for that nation only, but also that He would gather together in one the children of God who were scattered abroad.*
> *John 11:52*

Now this is true Worship:

The next day a great multitude that had come to the feast, when they heard that Jesus was coming to Jerusalem, took branches of palm trees and went out to meet Him, and cried out:

> *"Hosanna!*
>> *'Blessed is He who comes in the name of the Lord!'*
>> *The King of Israel!"*
>
> *John 12:12-14*

> *The Pharisees therefore said among them, "You see that you are accomplishing nothing. Look, the world has gone after Him!"*
> *John 12:19*

Therefore if worship was produced as a result of a miracle which had never been performed before (i.e.

after 4 days of death) and Lazarus still died a natural death afterwards; then think what to rise again never to die again brings. Only one has done this over 2000 years ago and **still lives today**. We know him through His Holy Spirit and the Word of God. This same Jesus, is the same saviour who has promised He will return for you and me. He has prepared a special place, a safe and secure place for you and me. We will reign with Him in splendour. We will judge angels. We will live in His glorious light forever. This is no fairy tale. Everyone's souls will last for eternity; those that perish will only know grief and eternal torment; those who are saved will know eternal righteousness, peace and joy in the Holy Ghost. Only believe and repent for He holds the keys to Death, Hades and to the Kingdom of God.

> *"I am He who lives, and was dead, and behold, I am alive forever, Amen. And I have the keys of Hades and of Death......"*
> *Revelations 1:18*

AMEN!

Truth

"Man can take away a person's possessions, reputation and dignity. But he cannot take away what was not his to give in the first place; and that is, **'The Ministry of Reconciliation**.'"

A saying by Tope Teniola (2007)

<u>STEAL</u>

Man took away Jesus' possessions. We took His clothes away as though to make Him poor and worthless.

> ***They divide My garments among them, and for My clothing they cast lots.***
> *Psalm 22:18*

<u>KILL</u>

Man took away His reputation. We discredited Him, lied about Him, gossiped about Him and disrespected Him.

> *.....Yet we esteemed Him stricken. Smitten by God, and afflicted.*
> *Isaiah 53:4b*

DESTROY

Man took away His dignity. As well as striping Jesus naked, we brutally flogged Him like an animal and nailed Him to the cross and left Him there for anyone in the world to watch Him die.

> .....*So His visage was marred more than any man. And His form more than the sons of men;.....*
> *Isaiah 52:14*

The source of our shameful actions is from the Thief, the Father of Lies, the Murderer from the beginning; Satan (John 10:10).

When man strips another man of His possessions, reputation and dignity, due to wickedness, he/she is joining with the enemy. He or she in order to feel empowered, will disempower another individual. The person being persecuted would naturally feel totally crushed inside. As it was never God's intention that man suffer pain of any kind, this would always hurt God. Hence, out of Jesus, our Lord and saviour's pain, the Ministry of Reconciliation was birthed. 2 Corinthians 5:17-21.

Joseph was striped of his heritage (Judaism), his belongings (including his precious coloured coat), his reputation and dignity. Yet because God was with him, his family and the whole of Israel were reconciled to him, hence to the Father in heaven, as they recognised God had not forsaken them in their suffering.

Today, the whole World is now being <u>reconciled</u> to the Father because what the devil meant for evil, God has turned into His good. Jesus Christ is the WAY, THE TRUTH AND THE LIFE. NO ONE COMES TO THE FATHER, EXCEPT THROUGH HIM.

Jesus did not entrust Himself to man prematurely because He knew what was in man's heart But at the right time, in order for scripture to be fulfilled, He handed Himself over to the authorities; for man's SALVATION.

That same man we crushed inside and outside, was buried and rose on the third day. He has been exalted to the highest place and is seated at the right hand of our Father in heaven. HE HAS TOTALLY FORGIVEN US. He will come again to judge the living and the dead. In the meantime, although we do not deserve it, He has prepared a special place for those who believe, to live with Him in heaven throughout eternity. Heaven and earth will indeed be restored to its former glory; evil will not be found.

Who is man? Number 6 is man's number. We are man. I am man. My sins also nailed Jesus to the cross (Romans 3:23). Out of man come evil thoughts. But Jesus warns us not to fear.

> *"And I say to you, My friends, do not be afraid of those who kill the body, and after that have no more they can do. But I will show you whom you should fear: Fear Him who, after He has killed, has power to cast into hell; yes, I say to you, fear Him!"*
> *Luke 12:4-5*

I have been at the receiving end of man's wickedness. I'm sure we all have at one stage of our lives. King David was accustomed to it.

> *The Lord is my light and my salvation; Whom shall I fear? The Lord is the strength of my life; of whom shall I be afraid? When the wicked came against me to eat up my flesh, My enemies and foes, they stumbled and fell. Though an army may encamp against me, My heart*

> *shall not fear; Though war may rise against me, in this I will be confident. One thing I have desired of the Lord, that will I seek: That I may dwell in the house of the Lord all the days of my life......*
> *Psalm 27:1-4*

David also was stripped of everything when he fled from the wrath of Saul. Even David who was innocent, chose to honour God by honouring Saul. He refused to touch God's anointed.

I have had people gossip about me and shamelessly long in their hearts to see me fall. But one thing man could not take; that which was not his to give me in the first place; the Ministry of Reconciliation. We are God's children. Our lives have been ordained as the foundations of the earth were being formed. Our Messiah, Jesus Christ, came to earth as a man but no sin was found within Him. All the rest of us are sinners. Those who are saved are saved sinners. Someone once said, "Evangelism is like one beggar showing another beggar where to find the bread."

I am that beggar today, beckoning those of you who have never given your lives to Christ or find yourselves in a backslidden condition and wish to rededicate your lives to Him; to you Jesus said:

"I am the bread of Life."

John 6:48

I point you today to the true bread. The people of Israel received manna from heaven daily but even that ran out; even the manna was temporary. They became hungry again. But there is One who always satisfies; One whose love does not run dry; His name is JESUS!

I received a further revelation about the powerful name of Jesus. Only recently, as I slept, in my dream a witch was trying to beckon me into a trap. In my spirit I cried out the name of JESUS, until the words actually came out of my mouth and the witch fled. You see, at the name of JESUS, Angels bow down; the earth bows down and so do demons and principalities. Philippians 2: 9-11. I urge you to use His name as your weapon against the enemy as he tries to steal, kill and destroy you. RISE UP, advance and attack with the weapon sharper than a double edged sword.

The Glory of God Descends -Revival

One of my visions mentioned in earlier chapters, is:

- To witness a Year of Jubilee/Personal Debt Cancellation in the UK, spreading to the entire World by 2050 *(Love & Forgiveness born through the fear of God, as in Leviticus 25 & Isaiah 61:2)*

This comes from a vision I had experienced. I was standing outside in the vision and saw the atmosphere around me changed colour into a kind of burnt orange; it was like millions of bright candles had been lit in a dark place. The odour of the atmosphere also changed into sweet smelling aroma. There was a feeling of love in the air as a dense bright fog fell like dew. I was filled with laughter, singing and dancing. Then I realised this was the glory of God descending upon the whole nation. Love and forgiveness was flowing through every creature, we did not have to work hard at it; it was easy and natural. People were letting go of debts owed and embracing one another in love. There was peace in the land and harmony among all men. It was the most beautiful thing I had ever experienced on earth, as I stood there in amazement and thanksgiving in my heart.

I truly believe the whole earth will experience this in my lifetime. There will be the greatest revival the world has ever known. It will be up to individuals to choose which way they go after this. There will be no excuse of ignorance. The Lord wants to show the World collectively, that He is the Lord God Almighty, the beginning and the end and there is no other. Our Father in heaven does not want any of His children to perish but to come to repentance, which leads to salvation.

Why the prayer of rededication? I rededicate my life to Jesus as long as I feel it is necessary. Any little backsliding is still backsliding. Even as ministers we are not perfect. Even stagnation can cause us to look away from our call. Jesus said, **"No one, having put his hand to the plough and looking back is fit for the kingdom of God." Luke 9:62.** God sees our heart. King David's prayer in Psalm 51 was more than a repentance prayer but a prayer of rededicating his life to the Lord. Do this from your heart, as many times as you need to. When you do, you will see the power of God working through you once again. (Below are my words but feel free to use your own).

THE PRAYER OF SALVATION/REDEDICATION

Dear Father,

I praise You, for You are the Alpha and Omega, the Great I Am. You know the end from the beginning and have the Master Plan.

I believe Jesus is the Son of God, who died to take away my sins and rose again on the third day and is seated at the right hand of the Father.

I am sorry when I thought I knew best; when I felt like giving up and refused to allow You to be Lord of my life.

I am sorry when I have walked in offence and bitterness and murmured against those I disagreed with, instead of taking my complaint to You. Please help me to walk in Love and Forgiveness for the rest of my life, as Christ forgave me.

I thank You, for I truly believe Your plan is to prosper me and not to harm me. Thank You for restoring hope for my future. Thank You for being patient with me and for not giving up on me. I thank You for Your tender mercies and unconditional love. I thank You for showing me Your ways are above mine. I thank You for reassuring me of belonging to You; for showing me I FIT PERFECTLY in You.

I thank You for preparing a special place for me where I can live with You throughout eternity. Please help me to endure on the journey to get there, and to overcome every obstacle.

Reign in my heart Lord; take Your rightful place on the throne of my life. For You alone do I trust to turn things around in my life, and not man.

'Create in me a pure heart O God, and renew a steadfast spirit within me. Restore to me the joy of Your salvation, and grant me a willing spirit to sustain me. Then I will teach transgressors Your ways and sinners will turn back to You.'

In Jesus' Name,
AMEN

WHO AM I IN CHRIST?

YOU FIT PERFECTLY!!!

THE BELL

I KNOW WHO I AM
I am God's child (John 1:12)
I am Christ's friend (John 15:15)
I am united with the Lord (1 Cor. 6:17)
I am bought with a price (1 Cor. 6:19-20)
I am a saint (set apart for God) (Eph. 1:1)
I am a personal witness of Christ (Acts 1:8)
I am the salt & light of the earth (Matt. 5:13-14)
I am a member of the body of Christ (1 Cor. 12:27)
I am free forever from condemnation (Rom. 8: 1-2)
I am a citizen of Heaven. I am significant (Phil. 3:20)
I am free from any charge against me (Rom. 8:31 -34)
I am a minister of reconciliation for God
(2 Cor. 5:17-21)
I have access to God through the Holy Spirit
(Eph. 2:18)

I am seated with Christ in the heavenly realms
(Eph. 2:6)
I cannot be separated from the love of God
(Rom. 8:35-39)
I am established, anointed, sealed by God
(2 Cor. 1:21-22)
I am assured all things work together for good
(Rom. 8:28)
I have been chosen and appointed to bear fruit
(John 15:16)
I may approach God with freedom and confidence
(Eph. 3: 12)
I can do all things through Christ who strengthens me
(Phil. 4:13)
I am the branch of the true vine, a channel of His life
(John 15: 1-5)
I am God's temple (1 Cor. 3: 16). I am complete in
Christ (Col. 2: 10)
I am hidden with Christ in God (Col. 3:3). I have been
justified (Romans 5:1)
I am God's co-worker (1 Cor. 3:9; 2 Cor. 6:1). I am
God's workmanship (Eph. 2:10)
I am confident that the good works God has begun in
me will be
perfected (Phil. 1: 5)
I have been redeemed and forgiven (Col.1:14) I have
been adopted as God's child (Eph.1:5)
I belong to God

TEN TIPS ON EXPERIENCING THE FATHER'S LOVE

I have prepared some practical tips on experiencing the Father's Love:

1. Every day you wake up, acknowledge God and thank Him for waking up alive and still in Him; also for your salvation;

2. Go to the Father in prayer, beginning with worship in spirit and in truth;

3. Have a heart of gratitude no matter what you are going through. Christ in you, the hope and glory;

4. Then have a moment of stillness and reflect and meditate on all those times from your childhood to now, when it was obvious the Lord had intervened in your life; (you can do this in quietness or with soft instrumental worship music playing in the background).

5. Start to thank Him for these times;

6. If you struggle to find positive things to meditate on, place one hand on your heart and ask God to take any stoniness/ hardness away from your heart and replace it with a supple heart. Read

Ezekiel 36:26-28; Isaiah 43:1-7 & 18-19; Jeremiah 31:3-4; and Colossians 2:10;

7. Confess unrepented sin, especially the sin of unforgiveness. Hebrews 4:16;

8. Meditate on the Cross, if it helps. We no longer have to sacrifice burnt offerings to get to the Father because Jesus is the Way, the Truth and the Life – we get to the Father through Jesus Christ, our only Saviour. John 14:6.

9. Start to receive and experience the Father's unconditional Love. He wants you to know how deep, how wide, how long, how high His Love is for you. Ephesians 3:18-19. He wants to tickle you and be your friend.

10. Thank Him again as He continues to fill you up to an overflowing.

Experience the receiving of the Father's love properly. Download His perfect love. If you let Him into your heart, you will learn He is the most beautiful loving DADDY you will ever know in your entire lifetime and throughout eternity. His Kingdom has no end; neither does His LOVE. The overflow of God's agape love is what you will want to give away to others as you walk in your call, with His grace upon you.

Any former distortion of God's Love will disappear and you will see He does not love us like man, with conditions attached.

For some of you, the above 10 tips will help instantly. However, for others, do not be discouraged if you do not feel a change straight away. The Holy Spirit who is the Spirit of Truth works on different people in different ways. Do not give up in wanting to receive the Father's Love daily.

I recommend my CD which has the poem: 'Love is like your Friend'. You can order this by emailing info@youfitperfectly.co.uk Like many others, you will be blessed.

※ ※ ※

❧ Bibliography ❧

Stibbe, Mark. *Prophetic Evangelism*. Authentic Media. Buckinghamshire, 2004.

Lamb, David. Angels & Demons. Marshall Pickering. London, 1999.

Bonnke, Reinhard UK Fire Conference 2007

Williams, Andrew and Stibbe, Mark. Breakout, Authentic Media. 2008

Chapman, Gary. The Five Love Languages - for Singles. Northfield Publishers, 2004

NKJV bible is used throughout this book, unless otherwise stated.

We invite you to continue your experience with the book
You Fit Perfectly at our website:

www.youfitperfectly.co.uk

- Share how you feel about the book You Fit
  Perfectly and read what others are saying

- Share your insights and discuss the book
  with other readers at the You Fit Perfectly
  Forum

- Communicate with the Author

- Purchase additional copies of You Fit
  Perfectly

- Write your inspired poetry or songs around
  the themes 'I know who I am' or 'I Fit
  Perfectly' and blog it

- Find out when and where the latest seminars
  and retreats based on the book will be held
  and how to book

For information about having the Author of You Fit
Perfectly speak to your church, organisation or group,
please send your emails to:

Email: info@youfitperfectly.co.uk

* * *